# 74 KEY LIFE SKILLS FOR A HAPPY SUCCESSFUL LIFE

## The Key Class
## Volume 2

**John J. Daly, Jr.**

www.trollriverpub.com
74 Skills for a Happy Successful Life
The Key Class
Copyright © 2015 John Daly
ISBN: 978-1-939564-70-2
Cover Design: Imran
Editor: Carol McKibben

Dear Reader,

John has worked very hard on this particular piece of entertainment. This book was brought to you by hard labor and love. Please respect an artist's work for the enrichment we try to bring you. I humbly ask that you don't outright steal this child born on paper and brought to you by love. If you come by this book by nefarious means, and you are simply unable to give the change in your pocket for the purchase price, then take it with my blessing. But if you can purchase it and would like John to continue to bring you great books, please purchase a copy to support him.

Thank you,
Troll River Publications

For information, contact johnkeyclass@gmail.com or
www.thekeyclass.com

# Dedication

This book is dedicated to my dear friend Carol McKibben without whom this book would not be possible.

With deep respect and love, John

# Contents

# INTRODUCTION

This book is a collection of articles written over the past 18 months. Each one represents a life skill that needs to be addressed if you are to be successful at anything – work, relationships or life.

It is divided into four basic sections: Behavior, Workplace Conduct, Image, and Interaction. To make it in this world, you have to not just fit in but also stand out. A paradox you think? Not really. Your behavior with others, no matter where you are will allow you to fit in. The image you project to others and the interaction you have with them will make you stand out.

Not convinced? Think you've got it all covered? I challenge you to read on and then decide.

# BEHAVIOR SKILLS

# Why Behavior Matters

From the time I was old enough to sit in a chair, my family gathered together to eat dinner around the same table. We had to make sure we were washed and clean for dinner promptly at 5:30 every afternoon. If for some reason a member of the family was going to have to be later, and it was not a one-time event, the hour was changed to meet that schedule. This was a very, very important part of our day. It was the time that we were taught table manners and, more importantly, how to carry on a conversation with others. This was when we all shared our day with each other. The conversation flowed and was spontaneous and had always happened this way from the time my siblings and I were very young. It was a time to get feedback from other members of the family about the issues we faced. It really was like a lesson in critical thinking as well as how to listen and practicing how to speak with other people. Talking with food in our mouths and arguing were not allowed. That's not to say we weren't allowed to debate. On the contrary, but it had to be thought out and respectful.

Little did I realize how much this was going to help me in my future. It was a huge boost for me when I started my first job with real consequence. I was able to sit with the head honchos and listen and yes comment on what was being said and done. It was because of doing this that I ended up breaking into the event world. As a designer in training, I was invited to the table when the American Institute of Floral Designers was formed. Why was a 19-year-old newbie allowed to converse with the big boys? They wanted fresh thinking. And, because those dinner lessons at the table taught me polite debate and listening skills I was taken seriously by those more experienced. My table manners were very good as well, and because of that I always had the advantage of looking like I belonged in any given circumstance that involved a meal. I had also learned the art of conversation and asking the right kind of "How and Why" questions. I learned that this was the easiest way to engage people. "Get them to talk about themselves, and they will always think you are very smart" was a mantra I learned from a young age. I also learned to respect others, which involved politeness, good manners and humility. I learned to be extremely observant and take initiative. Those grew out of the nightly dinners at home.

My first big break came along right after the AIFD formation meeting. The Teleflora Convention was being held at the newly-constructed Century Plaza Hotel in Los Angeles. (Yes, this was a very long time ago!) I went to all the planning meetings prior to the convention, not because I had to but I took the initiative to learn. The top designers from all over the country converged to construct the opening event in the ballroom under the direction of Teleflora. Unfortunately, there was a wait before construction could begin, and the people in charge got drunk! When I showed up, no one was there to direct. Not one to stand idly by, I jumped in and started ordering all the big name designers to begin the installation. No one questioned me! Two men stood watching me; soon they approached and offered me a drink. I politely declined and put them to work! The party was beautiful and a great success. In the end, the two men who had approached me were owners of a flower shop chain in Arizona. They offered me a job on the spot to run their new Tempe store. I went from designer in-training to manager! And, I owe it, and more, to those nightly dinners that taught me how to converse and treat others.

I have always learned best from listening to others. I questioned anything I did not understand. Because I wasn't a "book learner, I knew that I was not ever going to be able to tout a degree in anything. It was clear to me if I wanted to be respected and taken seriously I would have to act the part of success. That meant my behavior skills had to be tip-top. Thus began my fascination with North American etiquette, mostly pertaining to the United States, because I wanted to know why I was doing something rather than just doing it because I was told. I became fascinated with etiquette so much so that I started learning the customs and proper etiquette of other cultures I visited. Little did I realize this would lead me to owning an international company!

It's amazing how life teaches us what we need to know. I discovered that it is the little things that truly matter. In all my years of learning and working with etiquette, I have discovered that 70% of people who lose their jobs do so because they are unable to get along in their work environment, while only 30% lose a job from lack of knowledge or skill. This carries over to personal relationships as well. It's a hard statistic, and the reason I give you the first section of this book, Behavior Matters. It made a world of difference for me. Please take this to heart.

# 1
# Let's Start from the Beginning with Manners

Let's take a look at how bad behavior begins.

My wife and I were traveling recently. We'd gone to visit our relatives in Connecticut and decided to stay at a quaint hotel and take in some of the beautiful surroundings. It started the first night when after going to bed we heard children running up and down the hall, screaming. Fortunately, it was late and didn't last too long.

Unfortunately, it was only a brief respite! As we were enjoying our coffee the next morning, we were serenaded by the sound of a Big Wheel racing up and down the hall, followed by what sounded like stampeding horses and screeches and screams loud enough to permanently deafen us.

I stepped out into the hall to see two women leisurely leaning up against doors next to and across the hall from ours. They acted as if they were at a park outing as their children ran wildly about at 8 o'clock in the morning! I couldn't believe it! I looked at them and then their children, but they did nothing to cease the racket other than carry on their mindless conversation!

I gave them a rather stern look and started, "Excuse me, boys and girls, but you are old enough to be ladies and gentlemen and that means that you do not run up and down the halls in a hotel. There are other guests here, and this is not acceptable behavior."

With that the door directly across the hall from me flew open to reveal a man wrapped in a towel covered with shaving cream. He screamed, "Tyler, get your ass in the room now!"

Now I had a better understanding of why these kids behaved as they did. My parents never spoke in such a way to me nor did I ever speak to my children or grandchildren in that way. I have always said that if we show respect for others we are given respect by others. After my interaction, the mothers stood looking at me and then continued their conversation. It was an obvious case of "actions speak louder than words." If the mothers were willing to let their children treat the hall like a playground, why wouldn't they? And more importantly, when their children misbehave in the coming years, will they still continue to stand by and just let them do it?

What was wrong with that picture? Was it the fact that the children's mothers had failed to teach them consideration for others? Was it that the mothers themselves had no regard for the other guests? Was it that the father had no compunction about screaming a profanity at the children for all the other guests to hear? Obviously, since the adults in this situation saw nothing wrong with letting their children disturb others, they didn't have a clue about showing respect for others.

And therein is my point to you. While some parents have failed to take on the responsibility of teaching their children good manners and respect for others, it is most likely due to one of several reasons.

First, it is easier to let their children have their way than discipline and teach them. Parents' lives are filled with stress that overcomes everything else. Secondly, no one has every taught the parents the general good rules of society.

Having taught etiquette to more than 3,500 students in the last five years, I can honestly tell you that it boils down to those two issues. But, I can sincerely look you in the eyes and tell you that if we as a society don't make it a priority as part of parenting, we won't like the resulting adults that our grandchildren will become.

### The Keys to Teaching Children Good Manners

- Say what you mean, and mean what you say. Parents should always present a united front. Be consistent and stick to the rules you've outlined.
- No matter how busy, even if for 15 to 20 minutes, have dinner with your children. Over time, teach them table manners. Talk to them about their day and their problems and how to handle them.
- Show your children how to respect others. Do so by showing respect yourself. Start with demonstrating it with their grandparents, relatives and friends.
- Have them volunteer to help others less fortunate than they are. There are many, many causes that need help — everything from working at the homeless shelter serving meals or for a pet rescue to taking out the trash of an elderly neighbor or volunteering at any number of charities. Show them why they should be thankful for what they have.
- Teach them to say "please" and "thank you" and the occasions for which those words are appropriate.

It's all very basic but will set them on the right path to understanding how to show respect and good manners to others. And, it will mean the world of difference in their ability to be successful when they become adults.

# 2

# Life Is a Continuous Magic Act, So Never Disrupt or Disrespect

To drive home my point, I need to borrow from my dear friend, Andrea Michaels, founder and president of Extraordinary Events, a Los Angeles-based meeting and event planning and production firm. Every Friday for the last three years, she has published *The Good News Letter*. She created it on the premise that there is enough bad news in the world, and a publication filled with only "good news" would start everyone's weekend off in a positive way.

I recently read with interest one of her weekly editorials. It pulled on my heart strings and brightened my day. Did it have something to do with good manners? You know that it did!

So, with Andrea's permission, I share her column. It sends just the right, positive message for us all:

Last weekend my grandchildren reinforced a very important aspect of growing up ... good manners and consideration. We all went to The Magic Castle, which is open to kids only on weekends. I arrived early as did three women and various of their offspring. In a small waiting area, the key to entering the showrooms is to say "Open Sesame" to a closed door that will then open. One young girl repeated it over and over again to get the door to keep opening and closing while the mothers paid absolutely no attention. They intruded and disrupted all families who entered. The hostess politely asked the girl to stop doing that. The girl ignored her; the mothers said nothing.

Jon, Danielle and the boys (my son and his family) arrived. The disrupters were "inside." As we entered the first showroom, the kids allowed me to go first, or as both have learned, "Ladies always go first." The crew from the lobby was already inside, sitting in the front row, mothers nursing their cocktails in back. The kids were loud and raucous, and the moms laughed as if that was funny. Our boys were perfect gentlemen, as the magician took notice and commented.

On to another show with an amazing young magician, interrupted continuously by the rowdy and rude kids who disrespected not only the magician, but the entire audience by bouncing up to the stage, asking loud questions, and shouting ... you get the picture.

Every once in a while one of the moms would call out "Stop that (name)" and then howl hysterically. It went on for the entire show.

What's my point? Kids behave as they are taught to. When they are taught courtesy and consideration (as our boys have) they behave accordingly. When their role models are disrespectful of anyone and everyone, the kids behave as they see and hear. So it's our job to teach them right. We all need to treat each other with respect. Life is a continuous magic act ... filled with visions that spur imagination. It should never be disrupted or disrespected. Don't you agree? — Andrea Michaels

Magical words to my ears! I can't add anything that gets the message across better.

11

# 3
# Ode to Mother, and the Many Lessons She Taught Me

Andrea Michaels' message made me think of the life lessons my own mother taught me. I am a father and grandparent, but not too old to forget the life lessons that she taught me.

When my brother and I were young boys, our mother always had us make up our beds each morning. If we didn't make them correctly, she would pull everything off the beds and make us do them all over again. Her message to us was simple: "I hope you grow up to be men who have maids to make up your beds, and, if you are, you'll need to know if they are doing it correctly or not. If not, you will know how to keep your own house clean."

Understanding the simple tasks … how to do things for yourself … was something she instilled in us.

I put in a call to my brother and sisters today to reminisce what our mother taught us. We all remembered the following sayings that remain ingrained in us.

- Unto thine own self be true.
- To be loved, you have to be lovable.
- Where there is a will, there is a way.
- A job worth doing is worth doing well.

12

- Never be impertinent. (Does anyone even know what this means now?)
- Take time to smell the flowers. In other words, life is about more than YOU.
- Do not *ever* talk down to anyone.
- It can't hurt to ask; they can only say "no."
- You have to give to get.
- The more you put into it, the more you get out of it.
- Don't ever lie to me; tell me the truth, and I will help you figure out what to do.
- Life is 10 percent what you are given and 90 percent how you handle it.

Many of you might say that all this is just common sense. To me, this wise knowledge became the building blocks for my life. I still hear her voice in my head as these lessons frequently return to me. Interpret them as you will, but I think it all boils down to two things: how to be a kind and decent human being.

Thank you, Mom. I love you.

# 4
# Rudeness Is the Weak Man's Imitation of Strength

The boss raises his voice and loses his temper. A co-worker is unsupportive of your requests. A client uses her authority as a push factor to get things done. A manager is continually disrespectful. These are tough situations. Are they a result of poor parenting skills demonstrated previously? How should you handle them?

## Why Are People Rude?

First, let's look at some of the reasons why people are rude[2]. It's much easier for people to be rude over the phone, on the Internet or over email. Why? Because rude people often feel disconnected from others. That's why they lose it over petty things that won't matter in the next hour. Because they feel disconnected, in their minds, they have no reason to change that feeling. And when they are face-to-face with you, they have no idea why they should behave differently. While the Golden Rule (Do to others as you would have them do to you) should always apply, it often doesn't.

People often are rude because they are having a bad day, and misery loves company. Always remember that it is not your fault. Sometimes you can divert that bad mood by remaining calm and joking about something small. This often

14

brings out the rude person's need to vent, and in that case, just listen. This means overlooking the rudeness and talking to them. Perhaps they don't have anyone else to talk to, and you might just leave them feeling better.

Some people want to intimidate you into submission to appear stronger. It's the bully syndrome. Bullies are weak on the inside but don't want to show it. These are disconnected people. If you face them head-on, they often back down. This doesn't mean you become the bully, but rather that you face their behavior with them. Or, you can use the disarming technique[1] in the Video Resources Section of this book to see how it works.

Famous people like Simon Cowell have built their celebrity on being rude. Watching rude celebrities has become a national pastime. Again, these people are not connected with other people and only have an inflated sense of self. If we stop supporting the rude behavior of celebrities, they'll get the message. The same goes for people at work or in business who are chronic about rudeness. Stop enabling them.

### 4 Keys to Handling a Rude Co-Worker

- Don't lose your cool and don't take it personally.
- At the first occurrence, give the benefit of the doubt — try to cheer them up or be a good listener.
- Take it away from others; suggest grabbing a cup of coffee to discuss the issue privately to clear the air. If the person refuses to take it out of the workplace, say, "I can only imagine how frustrated you must be with this situation. Would you be willing to speak to me about it so I know how better to fulfill your expectations?" When you give angry people empathy, you take away their armor. You infer

that their rude behavior is not who they truly
are.

- If your authority or position is challenged, take
  the opportunity to privately get to the bottom of
  the issue. Say, "I can see you are terribly upset.
  Would you be willing to share with me what is
  bothering you so I can understand more fully
  how I might help you?

**What If It Is the Boss?**

If the boss explodes at you, remain calm and respectful.
Always give him the benefit of the doubt. Look him or her in
the eye and request a meeting to discuss the issue. When you
meet, ask the same question addressed in Point No. 4 above.

Consider this hypothetical situation. You ask the
question, and your boss confides that his wife is pregnant and
is having extreme morning sickness every day. This makes
him late. When he arrives, you are having a cup of coffee and
chatting with co-workers. It irritates him. Once you have this
knowledge, you will understand that his rudeness has nothing
to do with you, but you can do something that will improve his
mood. An example would be to buy a sweet roll and put it on
his desk when he arrives while saying, "I hope this gives you
a sweeter day." This will take the wind out of his sails.

I have used these techniques, and they have worked
extremely well for me.

# 5
# Social Media Creating a Less Civil Society

If you aren't convinced that rudeness prevails and that there is a need for everyone to be exposed to lessons in good manners, let our youth convince you. In the 40th Teen Trend Report released by StageofLife.com, and published by PRWeb, more than 5,500 junior and senior high school and college students revealed the factors leading to today's incivility. In the report, 92 percent of teens say that social media, including Facebook and Twitter, make us a less civil society. A whopping 70 percent of teens think society today displays more bad manners than good ones.

Students ranked family upbringing as the No. 1 factor affecting civility. Education level was No. 2, followed by socioeconomic status at No. 3.

The results revealed the following other statistics about teenagers and their views on manners:

- 47 percent have witnessed the most frequent rudeness and bad manners from school classmates compared to 6 percent from family at home, 27 percent from strangers in public places and 20 percent from friends and followers on social media.

- Students indicated that they learned "bad" manners from the media (69.3 percent), school (65 percent) and friends (61.5 percent). However, 43 percent named school as a positive influence on their manners, especially activities such as sports, student government, music and theater.
- What do teens claim as their biggest pet peeve? People being rude to cashiers, waiters and other service people that they've observed in public places.

These types of statistics, coupled with experienced observation, have inspired The Key Class to successfully provide behavior training to students in the high schools and other programs like the United Way of Santa Barbara, the Workforce Investment Board of Santa Barbara County and the county Juvenile Services Division.

In addition to the 5,500 students responding to the survey, an additional 125 teen bloggers submitted an essay to StageofLife.com sharing personal stories and thoughts about civility that answered the question, "Where has civility gone?" The winning first-place student essay was entitled, "Not the Same as Respect," and was written by a South Korean high school student. A URL for the Essay is provided in the Reference section at the end of this book.

A Twitter contest, tied into the monthly question about civility, selected a winner. It came from @MissMelBell98, who wrote, "Civility is fleeting fast because people are no longer expected to have it, so in turn, we don't have anything to live up to."

I'm proud to say that the site collaborated with international etiquette expert, Jay Remer, "The Etiquette Guy" (and my friend), to craft and judge the writing contest. Remer is the acting Etiquette Coach for StageofLife.com, where he answers real-life questions about manners and civility in the etiquette advice sections of the website.

# 6
# Social Media Missteps that Will Haunt You Forever

Because we are either sitting in front of a computer or focused on our cell phones and not looking at others face-to-face, it is often easy to fall into what I call "social media pitfalls." These are the habits that we fall into without thinking it through. Everything is so fast-paced these days that it's easy to fall into specific traps.

What's important to remember is that once something goes out on the Internet, i.e. social media, it is there for all the world to see. At some point, what you've posted may come back to haunt you, whether it is a prospective hiring manager checking you out or someone who may be interested in you personally.

The following pitfalls will leave a negative impression that you may not mean to convey. Let's examine them:

- Airing personal dislikes related to politics, religious beliefs, wealth vs. poverty, obesity, or eating disorders. It is best to avoid these topics.
- Telling off-color jokes or using profanity. Doing so paints you as a rude and inconsiderate person who offends others.
- Criticizing others about their appearance, beliefs or behavior. It is best not to criticize

20

those who are offensive but rather defend those being criticized if you must get involved. Rule of thumb is to avoid involvement.

- Commenting about race, sexual behavior, gambling and drinking, guns and weapons, drug use, gender-related humor or poking fun at the disabled. These are taboo.

- Relating personal or confidential information about yourself or others, such as reporting a death in someone's family, an illness of another, or a pregnancy, etc. Let those involved handle them. Even if you are reporting about yourself, it is best not to use social media to announce these issues. It's more appropriate to discuss them in person (or over the phone if distance is an issue) with those close to you. Once it is common knowledge, then allow discussion on social media if you so choose.

- Providing a blow-by-blow status of what you are eating, where you are going (on a day-to-day basis) or that you are sitting on the sofa with your significant other. No one cares and this soon becomes irritating to others.

- Publishing photos of others, using location-based tagging, or even tagging the names of others in public updates without permission. Respect the privacy of others.

- Using social media to rant and rave. Don't use it to rant about the horrible customer service of a restaurant or company. Social media isn't your own personal soapbox, and it really makes you look petty when you do so.

- Presenting an overall negative demeanor or "voice" on social media. Don't be like Debbie Downer on *Saturday Night Live*. No one likes to be brought down on a continuous basis, and you'll find yourself "defriended" more often than not.

It's best to always convey a positive, upbeat and respectful "persona" on social media. People like to be around happy and positive. That goes for business and life! Keep it in mind the next time you sign on!

# 7
## Etiquette Coaches Revel Top Etiquette Flaws

A year ago I polled a number of my peers to determine what they saw as the top mistakes made by their clients. Here's what we collectively formulated based on our experience with customers.

- Lack of cell phone etiquette
- Not knowing how to make proper introductions and greetings
- Not enough consideration for others, leaving the "golden rule" on life support
- Poor handshakes
- Poor dining etiquette
- Not understanding how to appreciate
- Not knowing how to say goodbye
- Conversing and networking in a group in front of a buffet table
- Ignoring RSVP requests to invites
- Not understanding the importance of small talk or how to develop this skill set
- Not listening and interrupting people during conversation

- Not knowing the basic etiquette of being the "host" or the "guest"
- Disrespecting others
- Being too self-absorbed
- Diving straight into business with no "warm-up" social talk
- Eating and talking on the phone at the same time
- Talking so loudly in a restaurant that most diners can hear the conversation
- Having a roving eye when the conversation is deemed to be of no value to the listener
- Lack of "thank you" and "you're welcome"
- Lack of techno etiquette

Did you notice that these ALL boil down to not having consideration for other people? The keys here are lack of respect and self-respect. One colleague made note that the Oxford Dictionary chose "selfie" as the word of the year for 2013 and pointed out that this is incredibly telling.

Many people feel that they have a handle on proper behavior, when, in fact, 76 percent of adults believe Americans are ruder and less civilized than they were 20 or 30 years ago. A link to 2012 survey results on bad manners is listed in the Reference section at the end of this book.

The lesson in all of this is simply to put consideration for others at the top of your list. If you are guided by this one simple rule, people will truly see you as a real role model.

# 8
# The 11 Traits of a Respectful Person Equal Success

In working with teens, I've found that it clearly helps them get a grip when they understand why being respectful matters. Too often we assume they know these things when they actually don't.

This was brought into sharp focus in a recent class I was teaching. In this case, actions spoke much louder than words. Kids were texting and talking among themselves on top of not watching me while I was teaching. One boy was sleeping. Several were even rolling their eyes. This was the last straw.

"This class is about respect[3] for people as much as it's about learning the basics of a good handshake," I said.

I was firm and direct. I came down on them without talking down to them.

"How would you feel if you were in my place as the teacher and, with my body language, I let you know I couldn't care less about what you were saying?"

They all agreed that, as they put it, "It sucks the way we're acting." I explained to them that I have a lot of respect for them and what they are going through during this time in their lives.

25

"I'm only trying to help you and ask for the same respect back from all of you."

I stressed how we can have conversations or disagreements with respect for each other without yelling or talking down, and that was what I was trying to illustrate to them at that moment. I smiled and announced, "Next time someone falls asleep in class, I'll ask him to excuse himself and go to the office to take a nap." It was important for them to know what I wouldn't tolerate.

Next, I challenged them with, "What do you think are the qualities of a respectful person?"

The comments were, "Respect your elders, be nice, blah, blah, blah."

My response: "Really? You think respect is only about being nice to your elders? Boy, have I got some details for you! Let's look at the traits of a respectful person and how having them will get you what you want in life."

**Trait No. 1:** They're honest. They don't lie. People can depend on them. Think of the heroes we admire in books, movies and real life. Don't they act with honesty and integrity?

**Trait No. 2:** They don't lose their tempers, scream, yell or strike out against others when things don't go their way. In other words, they rarely lose control. When negative things happen to them, they remain positive. They treat people as they would like to be treated.

**Trait No. 3:** They are tenacious. They don't give up easily. They become resourceful when the going gets rough. They totally get that they can't change other people or the circumstances, but that they can change their attitudes about situations.

**Trait No. 4:** They admit when they're wrong. Instead of sticking to their guns (no matter what) just to be "right," they fess up to their mistakes, particularly when it lets another person "off the hook" or eases a situation.

**Trait No. 5:** They aren't lazy; they strive. They are hard workers who always want to "get it right."

**Trait No. 6:** They have their priorities straight. They put what is truly important, what will really help others or a situation, above their own needs.

**Trait No. 7:** They have an inner sense of right and wrong. They innately know the right thing to do, and they understand clearly when an injustice is being served.

**Trait No. 8:** They tend to be role models for other people. Others admire and look up to them.

**Trait No. 9:** They are givers. Most successful people are. They know the "secret" that the more you give, the more you receive when you are genuine about your gifts. We're talking not so much about money but time and expertise. They operate on Zig Ziglar's quote, "You will get all you want in life if you help enough people get what they want."

**Trait No. 10:** They have high self-esteem. They believe they deserve success and know they can do anything they go after. They know that a mistake is something they do and not who they are. They keep a positive self-image because they know that self-esteem is a state of mind that they have chosen.

**Trait No. 11:** They are loyal, even when it's tough to be. They stand behind those with whom they have forged relationships and don't betray them.

At this point, my students were all listening intently. I explained further. "If a person has all these traits, how will that help him be successful? Isn't it obvious? These are the qualities of highly successful people in our society — I'm talking Bill Gates, Oprah, Warren Buffet, George Washington, Abraham Lincoln and the like. It isn't a coincidence that both highly respected and highly successful people possess these traits."

The student who fell asleep raised his hand and asked, "So, by being a respectful person and having the traits you listed, success will find me?"

"Exactly," I replied. "Like an oncoming train!"

# 9

# Lying and the Importance of Being Earnest

Picking up on Trait No. 1, above, let's look at lying and the importance of being earnest. No, this isn't about the farcical comedy in which the protagonists maintain fictitious personae to escape their social obligations. But somehow, that fits with being honest.

Let's start with a hard look at honesty. Simply put, it means to truthfully provide information when asked, including what you did or did not do, or what someone else did or did not do. It means not leaving out important facts to shield the complete truth. And, it means admitting mistakes if you've made them. In keeping with the title of this piece, it also means not pretending to be someone or something that you are not.

## Why Does Honesty Matter?

The first big reason is that it creates trust. It means that when you do make a mistake, people are more likely to forgive you and give you a second chance. Everyone makes mistakes. Lies on top of them only lead to more problems and will paint a person as dishonest. It's very much like the boy who cried wolf too many times as a joke. When the wolf appeared, no one would believe him.

Being honest also builds confidence. When you are truthful, you can be assured that you can be confident in what you are saying. Personal development is about fostering positive qualities within yourself. Honesty enables you to rid feelings of negativity that hold you back personally and professionally.

It allows you to live a life of integrity, showing your true self to others. It shows others that you are reliable, genuine.

## The Facts about Dishonesty

Being completely honest can be very difficult. Lying often appears to be the easiest "out" for a situation. But, once you have been untruthful, and you are discovered (trust me, lies are always uncovered), the consequences will make your situation 10 times worse.

Dishonesty is about concealment and living your life in the shade. It holds back growth. It adds an element of mystery that others sense as dishonesty. Even the best liars on earth will attract only similarly dishonest people and be on the receiving end of the dishonesty of others.

Let's take a look at a hypothetical. You are in a position of opportunity in your career or another situation attached to money or power. You're a basically good and honest person who on occasion has turned a "blind eye" or "held back with the truth" in order to gain something. However, if you really respect yourself, you'll discover that later you feel badly because you got ahead through dishonest means. So, your conscience starts to "beat you up" over your own dishonesty. In the long run, these weren't gains at all.

## White Lies

We've all told white lies because brutal honesty might inflict pain or distress on another. For instance, Mary told Tim she couldn't go out with him on Saturday night because she and her family were going out of town. You are Mary's best friend and know it is because she doesn't find Tim attractive and doesn't want to date him.

When Tim asks you if the reason is genuine, what do you say? Do you want to be brutally honest and tell Tim the truth or tell him you don't know if it is genuine or not to spare Tim's feelings? Perhaps in this instance it is better to be economical with the truth and just say you think Mary has other plans. This isn't the complete truth, but you are sparing Tim's feelings on something that won't have a real impact on his future.

However, this is one of those instances where you need to clearly think it through. Some would advise you to very gently let Tim know that Mary isn't really interested in him rather than saying something that will make matters worse. While you never want to hurt someone, there may be a diplomatic solution in which you tell Tim the truth and let Mary know about the conversation. She will probably be grateful that you ended her white lie, and both parties can move on with their lives.

Finally, the truth really does set you free. Being someone that others can count upon to be both open and earnest will be returned to you in the respect and honesty you will receive from others.

# 10
## Ethically Speaking ... It Was the Right Thing to Do

Consider that honesty should always be paired with ethics.

I had an interesting exchange with a vendor that I wanted to share with you. The vendor had performed services for me more than a month ago. I anticipated the bill to be close to $800.

The vendor had performed the same service for a neighbor of mine the day after he had worked at my house. This past weekend, I was having a casual conversation with my neighbor, and it occurred to me that I hadn't yet received a bill from our mutual vendor. That thought prompted me to ask my neighbor if he'd received his bill for the work the vendor had done for us. He responded that he had received it on Monday of last week.

I scratched my head on that one and wondered why I hadn't received the bill, which the vendor had indicated would be mailed at the end of the past month. So, I called the vendor and asked his assistant about the missing bill.

She did a computer search and couldn't find any pending or recent billing for me. I asked her to check on it and let me know. I told her to feel free to just email me with the invoice, and I would make sure the bill was paid immediately.

31

The assistant paused on that one, and said, "Mr. Daly, I am amazed that you would call us to follow up on something that is clearly our error. If you hadn't called, most likely you wouldn't have been billed for our services. You are a very honest man."

My immediate response? "I wouldn't feel good about cheating someone out of money rightfully owed to him."

Her comment? "That is rare indeed. Thank you for calling and bringing this to our attention."

This leads me to the topic of ethics. Ethics and good manners go hand-in-hand. It really goes back to that good ole' Golden Rule of treating others as you would like to be treated. If you had been that vendor, made a mistake in billing and ended up not getting paid, wouldn't you want your customer to treat you honestly?

It saddens me that my vendor's assistant felt it rare that people wouldn't be honest about a billing mistake.

What are your thoughts? Would you have called the vendor and asked for a missing bill? Tell me via johnkeyclass@gmail.com.

# 11
## Making Ethical Choices Matters

Ethics is <u>NOT</u>
- Always doing everything correctly
- Never making mistakes
- Never doing anything we would regret
- Never missing paying a bill
- Never saying anything that is not proper

What Ethics <u>IS</u>
- Recognizing our mistakes
- Making amends for mistakes
- Reversing the damage of our behavior
- Explaining truthfully why we missed paying a bill
- Apologizing to someone that we have hurt with words written or spoken
- Not sharing harmful information with others

The temptation to work in an unethical manner can be great, especially when it promises financial gain. These are the times to dig deep and ask lots of questions. Is the gain worth it in the long run? Will I be able to trade this action for my good reputation? Where will this put me in 20-30 years?

For example, when I was working in the event industry, I had a freelance designer that I had worked with for a number of years. We had a wonderful relationship, and I called on him for almost every one of my jobs. On one project, with a client with whom we worked all of the time, the client asked him for his phone number as she had several small projects with shoestring budgets about which she wanted to contact him directly and did not want to hire him through my company. He gave her his number, and she began calling him for jobs. The jobs got larger, and he did more décor for her. Soon he improperly installed a prop in the ceiling of a ballroom, and it was not secure. Because he was just a freelancer, he did not carry any type of insurance. The prop fell and caused damage to the property. Of course, the client was sued for damages, and I ultimately learned what had happened. As a result, the freelancer was no longer called to work with my staff and ended up having to pay back to the client far more than he could have ever earned with her on her "little" jobs to cover the damage. Whenever I was asked for a recommendation on his work, I warned people he was not to be trusted. As for the client, I fired her! As you can see, the freelancer's unethical behavior cost him not only future work with me but with the client and other prospective customers in the future.

Over the years, I have always worked with very high ethical standards, and it has paid many dividends. My clientele were people with whom I worked for anywhere from 5 to 30 years. Ninety-eight percent of my work was from repeat business. I never had to advertise but was fortunate to have business come to me. I enjoyed 44 years in the world of special events, and, I retired with no regrets. So many of my great friends have come from that business, and I still relish in the fact my reputation is untarnished, because I made ethical behavior one of my top priorities.

In today's world, there are so many available resources and classes for businesspeople to take to ensure ethical professionalism. They easily can be found through colleges and universities and professional organizations. However the bottom line relies within each of us. When you are faced with a decision that you know in your heart is wrong, go with that feeling. Please use the Golden Rule: Do onto others as you would have them do unto you. You can't go wrong if you do.

# 12
# How to Deal with the "Silent Treatment"

Sometimes we have to deal with dishonest or unethical behavior from friends. Let's look at one scenario and how to handle it.

Let me set the scene. A good friend doesn't return your voice or text messages. Your emails go unanswered. You get no response whatsoever. This comes out of the blue. You scratch your head and try to figure out what's happened.

Has this ever happened to you? If so, what did you do? Did the relationship fall by the wayside? Yes, you are being treated unfairly, but if the friendship is worth saving, what can you do to resolve it?

### Consider Your Recent Behavior
Put some thought into what you might have done to cause your friend to be upset with you. Could your words or actions have been misinterpreted? Reflect on recent events. That may shed some light on what created the problem.

### Ask Your Friend If You've Done Something to Cause a Problem
First of all, your friend's behavior may have nothing to do with you. Don't make assumptions that you have caused a problem. Don't let anxiety or tension grow within you. As

quickly as you can, catch up with your friend and ask him or her point blank if everything is all right. That will immediately break the tension.

When you ask, you may discover that your friend's mood change has nothing to do with you. That's the time to be a real friend and help with the problem. Give your friend the chance to be honest and open up about the issue if there is one.

If you actually are the cause of your friend's behavior, apologize for any misunderstanding you may have created. Use the words, "I apologize. I did not mean to hurt you. Please forgive me."

### Give Your Friend Some Space
Once you have ascertained the problem and either apologized or provided a shoulder to lean on, give your friend some space if he or she needs it. What happens next is in your friend's hands. You reached out and made the effort to make everything right with him or her. It's up to your friend to take the next step.

### Don't Discuss This with Others
This is a personal matter between you and your friend. It is only natural that you may want to turn to another friend for support. Don't. Always sort this out with the person giving you the cold shoulder. If you go to others, you just create tension and most likely gossip among your other friends. That will only make matters worse.

### Don't Challenge or "Push" Your Friend
If after approaching your friend, he or she doesn't want to talk about your concerns, don't make matters worse by challenging or pushing for an answer. That will create more tension. If your friend tells you that nothing is wrong, take it on face value. Drop it. You've reached out and shown that you care and are concerned by the behavior. Understand that you did your best to assuage the situation.

### Don't Withdraw from Your Friend

You've reached out, shown your concern and apologized if need be. If you are told that everything is "fine," try to set up a time to go out and have some fun together. Laughter is great medicine. It will be easier for your friend to loosen up and either confide in you or forgive you, whichever is needed. If your friend claims to have no time to "hang" with you, then something major is going on under the surface.

Keep in mind that not everyone will respond to problems the way you do. Some people take more time than others. At this point, give your friend time and space. Like the song says, "If you love someone, set them free." If they love you, they'll come back to you when they are ready.

It's all about the effort that you make that will leave a lasting impression on others.

# 13
# Nothing Replaces Persistence as a Formula for Success

Are you focused on being successful? A blog written by my associate, Carol McKibben, really captured my interest. It outlined how her persistence had brought her success in life.

I have numerous friends who, through hard work and persistence, have achieved great success. I think President Calvin Coolidge stated it best in his famous quote:

"Nothing in this world can take the place of persistence. Talent will not; nothing is more common than unsuccessful people with talent. Genius will not; unrewarded genius is almost a proverb. Education will not; the world is full of educated derelicts. Persistence and determination alone are omnipotent. The slogan 'press on' has solved and always will solve the problems of the human race."

I know that my own persistence has taken me further than I had anticipated. This all got me to thinking about how does a person become persistent? If not really inclined to do so, what will give individuals the ability to develop persistence?

Here's the action plan:

- **Set a definite goal or purpose**

This needs to be backed up by a burning desire to fulfill the goal.

- **Develop a definite plan**

It never hurts to write your plan out. What steps will it take to get from A to Z and achieve the goal? Follow each step to completion — all the way through from beginning to end.

- **Keep a positive attitude**

Along with that goes a mind that is tightly closed to negativity. Don't let self-doubt or setbacks stop you. Even if everyone around you is telling you "it can't be done."

- **Create friendly alliances**

Surround yourself with people who believe in you and your dreams. Find people who will encourage you, support you and help you follow through with both plan and purpose.

Don't take my word for it. This action plan above is paraphrased from Napoleon Hill's best-seller, *Think and Grow Rich.*

Originally published in 1937 and inspired by a suggestion from Scottish-American businessman Andrew Carnegie, the title implies that the book deals with how to get rich. According to Hill, however, the philosophy taught in his book can be used to help people succeed in all lines of work and do or be almost anything they want. (Note: By 2011, this book had sold more than 70 million copies.)

What I've outlined above is part of the essence of the book. It's worked for millions of people. Why not you?

## 14
## Famous People and the "Simple Secrets" to Success

I've been thinking about how I can impress on our young people the simple secrets to success.

It is simple, right? There is no magic formula. Just hard work, persistence and knowing that at any given point in life things will change. In other words, "This too shall pass." Hard times and good times don't last forever.

I know. I've been there. Each of us can easily flub up the "good times." At the same time, we can pull ourselves up by our bootstraps and go from the bottom to the top.

Don't take my word for it! Here are some practical, true-life stories that support the theory that hard work, persistence and knowing that "this too will pass" are the simple secrets to success!

- Bill Gates, CEO of Microsoft, dropped out of Harvard to start his company. He had an idea what he was getting into. People like to believe he was the "Right man at the Right place at the Right time." But he worked hard and didn't give up his dream.
- Michael Jordon had prodigious physical gifts. But as his long-time coach Phil Jackson wrote: "It was hard work that made him a legend.

41

When Jordan first entered the league, his jump shot wasn't good enough. He spent his off-season taking hundreds of jumpers a day until it was perfect." In a piece at NBA.com, Jackson writes that Jordan's defining characteristic wasn't his talent, but having the humility to know he had to work constantly to be the best.

- Cy Young Award-winning pitcher Roy Halladay is one of the hardest-working men in baseball. According to *Sports Illustrated*, he routinely puts in a 90-minute workout before his teammates make it to the field. His former pitching coach told *SI* that when other pitchers attempted one of his workouts, none of them could complete half of it.

- *American Idol* host Ryan Seacrest told the *New York Times* that even as a young child, his goal was to be a "a classic iconic broadcaster." He's moved toward that goal by taking on a preposterous workload. In addition to hosting *American Idol*, Seacrest appears seven days a week on *E!*, hosts a daily radio show from 5 to 10 a.m., appears on the *Today* show, runs a television production company, and recently received $300 million in private-equity funding to acquire more businesses.

- Yahoo! CEO Marissa Mayer is known for her incredible stamina and work schedule. She used to put in 130 hour weeks at Google. She told Joseph Walker of *The Wall Street Journal* that she managed that schedule by sleeping under her desk and being "strategic" about her showers. Even people critical of her management style acknowledge that she "will literally work 24 hours a day, seven days a week." That paid off with one of the biggest jobs in technology.

- At first glance, the amazing success of Dallas Mavericks owner and entrepreneur Mark Cuban looks like a stroke of luck. He sold his first company at the peak of its value, and got into technology stocks at exactly the right time. Cuban writes on his blog that it took an incredible amount of work to benefit from his luck. When starting his first company, he routinely stayed up until 2 in the morning reading about new software, and went seven years without a vacation.

- Steve Jobs left incredibly big shoes for Tim Cook to fill at Apple. However, the man got the top job for a reason. He had always been a workaholic. *Fortune* reports that he began sending emails at 4:30 in the morning. A profile in Gawker revealed that he was the first in the office and last to leave. He used to hold staff meetings on Sunday night in order to prepare for Monday.

- While Henry Ford is today known for his innovative assembly line and American-made cars, he wasn't an instant success. In fact, his early businesses failed and left him broke five times before he founded the successful Ford Motor Company.

- Today Disney rakes in billions of dollars from merchandise, movies and theme parks around the world, but Walt Disney himself had a bit of a rough start. He was fired by a newspaper editor because, "he lacked imagination and had no good ideas." After that, Disney started a number of businesses that didn't last too long and ended with bankruptcy and failure. He kept plugging along, however, and eventually found a recipe for success that worked.

- Most people know Oprah as one of the most iconic faces on TV as well as one of the richest and most successful women in the world. Oprah faced a hard road to get to that position, however, enduring a rough and often abusive childhood as well as numerous career setbacks, such as being fired from her job as a television reporter because she was "unfit for TV."

- Just about everybody knows who Jerry Seinfeld is, but the first time the young comedian walked on stage at a comedy club, he looked out at the audience, froze and was eventually jeered and booed off of the stage. Seinfeld knew he could do it, so he went back the next night, completed his set to laughter and applause, and the rest is history.

- While today Steven Spielberg's name is synonymous with big budget, he was rejected from the USC film school three times. He eventually attended school at another location, only to drop out to become a director before finishing. Thirty-five years after starting his degree, Spielberg returned to school in 2002 to finally complete his work and earn his BA.

- J.K. Rowling may be rolling in a lot of *Harry Potter* dough today, but before she published the series of novels she was nearly penniless, severely depressed, divorced, trying to raise a child on her own while attending school and writing a novel. Rowling went from depending on welfare to survive to being one of the richest women in the world in a span of only five years through her hard work and determination.

- As one of the best-selling artists of all time, Elvis Presley has become a household name even years after his death. But back in 1954, Elvis was still a nobody, and Jimmy Denny, manager of the Grand Ole Opry, fired him after just one performance telling him, "You ain't goin' nowhere, son. You ought to go back to drivin' a truck."

- In his first film, Harrison Ford was told by the movie execs that he simply didn't have what it takes to be a star. Today, with numerous hits under his belt, iconic portrayals of characters like Han Solo and Indiana Jones, and a career that stretches decades, Ford can proudly show that he does, in fact, have what it takes.

My point isn't to get our youth to work 24/7. But even if this persistent work ethic inspires them to have a "yes, I can attitude" and a will to succeed, then they will have adopted the simple secrets to success.

# 15
# The Benefits of a Positive Attitude

I started thinking about the benefits of positive thinking on a recent morning, especially how it relates to achieving success. Two thoughts popped into my mind:

- A positive attitude convinces you that you can achieve success.
- A negative attitude makes you believe that you cannot achieve success.

I once spoke to three highly successful people and asked them why they thought they had succeeded in such spectacular ways. All of them answered with this same response in one form or another: I never considered that I couldn't succeed!

If you have a positive attitude, it is manifested in:

- Positive thinking
- Constructive thinking
- Creative thinking
- Optimism
- The motivation and energy to do things and accomplish goals
- An attitude of happiness

That same positive attitude creates:

- Expectation of success and not failure

- Inspiration
- Happiness
- The strength not to give up if you encounter obstacles on your way
- A belief that failure and problems are blessings in disguise
- Belief in yourself and in your abilities
- The achievement of your goals and success
- Self-esteem and confidence
- Refusal to dwell on problems; instead, you look for solutions
- The ability to see and recognize opportunities
- Better interaction with everyone around you, whether they are part of your team or are customers
- More love and respect from others

A positive attitude results in happiness and success. It helps you cope more easily with everyday life. It affects your entire environment and everyone around you. It's contagious! And it truly can change your life.

### Simple Tips to Develop a Positive Attitude

Remez Sasson, founder of successconsciousness.com, is an author teaching how to use mental tools and inner powers to create a life of happiness, success, fulfillment and inner peace. He offers the following tips for developing a positive attitude:

- Choose to be happy. Yes, it is a matter of choice. When negative thoughts enter your mind, just refuse to look at them, substituting them with happy thoughts.
- Look at the bright side of life. It's a matter of choice and repeated attempts.
- Choose to be optimistic.

- Find reasons to smile more often. You can find such reasons, if you look for them.
- Have faith in yourself, and believe that the Universe can help you.
- Associate yourself with happy people.
- Read inspiring stories.
- Read inspiring quotes.
- Visualize only what you want to happen, not what you don't want.

Trent Hamm at The Simple Dollar offers up five tactics to improve your attitude:

**1. Come up with a positive response to every situation you meet**

Yes, sometimes our first response is negative. I'm never happy when my daughter uses too much toilet paper and proceeds to flood the bathroom, for example. Simply stepping back for a moment and looking for a positive response to the situation can make all the difference. The spilled water can be a close experience with my daughter, as I gather up some towels to mop up the water and allow her to help me as we sing songs while doing it, then I plunk her in the tub as I Lysol the floor, and then we have a fun bath time.

**2. Look for the good in other people**

Rather than seeking to identify the negative traits in the people around you that you interact with, look for the positive ones. Person A might not be the most skilled person, but he does put forth a lot of effort and asks a lot of good questions. Person B might have a caustic personality, but she does show tremendous efficiency in handling some incredibly complicated projects.

**3. Act happy, even if it's a painted dayglow smile**

You don't have to be happy — often, that's an impossibly tall order. Instead, just act happy. The more you do it, the more natural it becomes. Even more interesting, the more you do it, the more it becomes a part of you — you actually do feel happier.

### 4. Drop the sarcasm

Sarcasm can be a lot of fun, but in the end, it's just negativity wrapped up and packaged as a joke. Drop the sarcasm — you don't need to ridicule things you don't like. Just expend your energy elsewhere; don't even think of the ridicule-worthy things at all.

### 5. Get plenty of rest and eat a good diet

This (along with exercise) is one sure way to naturally elevate your mood. It'll increase your energy and focus, decrease your stress, and make it easier to interact with the world.

You have nothing to lose and everything to gain by adding a little more positivity to your life.

# 16
## How to Stress Someone Out with Your Cell Phone

Even if you have a positive attitude, others might spoil it with negative actions. Here's an example.

It's a great evening. You're having dinner with a friend. You are just about to tell your friend about this amazing new job opportunity. Just part way through the lead-up to your exciting news, your friend's cell phone rings. He holds up his finger, stopping you in midsentence, and answers the phone. You've lost him. He's off on another conversation with someone else, and he stays on the phone for more than 10 minutes. You become bored, somewhat agitated and more than a little stressed out.

Has this ever happened to you? Have you been on either side of the table? Do you wish you had a list of rules to follow when it comes to cell phones? Probably not, but I'm going to give them to you anyway. If you don't want to be rude, hurt someone else's feelings or stress them out, use this list to temper your behavior with your cell phone.

- Don't order food or drinks while on your cellphone. If you're in a line and your phone rings just when it is your turn to order, don't carry on a conversation. Don't answer the phone until after you've completed your order. Why? Because if you are having a conversation and ordering at the same time, you are being rude to your server and inconsiderate to those in line behind you. Return the call after you are out of line.

• Don't keep checking your cell phone during dinner with family or friends. How do you feel when you're having a conversation and the other person pulls out his or her cell phone and checks it? You might as well set off a flare gun that signals you aren't really listening to the other person. If this is a problem, leave your cell phone in the glove compartment of your car!

• When you are with your children, don't look at your phone. If you keep fiddling with your phone while they are trying to get your attention, you are teaching them a) that someone else is more important than they are and b) that this is the behavior they should imitate.

• If you are having a fantastic experience, stay focused on the experience and not taking a photo of it with your cell phone camera. Learn to be in the here and now and enjoy it. Once you have, then get out your phone and take a picture.

• During meetings, movies or large events, put your phone on silent. Do you realize how disruptive and annoying you being on your phone can be to others? If something urgent occurs, silence your phone, leave the meeting, movie or event and call back once you are in a quiet place where you won't disturb others.

- Never ever use your phone while driving. It is as worse as drinking and driving, and responsible for just as many accidents. If you must use your phone, pull over, stop the car and make or answer a call. The same goes for walking and texting on your cell phone. Don't walk down the sidewalk playing Angry Birds and not look where you are going. It could mean a trip to the hospital, or worse.

- If you are getting a haircut, a manicure or interfacing with a service person, don't be disrespectful to the professional providing you service by talking on your phone. Put your phone on airplane mode and leave it there until the professional has finished providing you the service.

Cell phones didn't become popular until 1998. We were all able to somehow live without them up until then. Putting them aside for an hour or two won't be the end of the world.

Cell phones are great convenience factors, but they can have good and bad applications. For many it becomes a source of stress instead of a helpful tool.

# 17
# The Consequences of Being Late

Do you know co-workers who are always late? Are you chronically late? Do you or someone you know show up late for work, to meetings, for phone conferences, for social gatherings? I doubt seriously that you would consider that something anyone does on purpose. In reality, it's simply a lack of time-management skills. It's the lack of realization that you are valuing your own time over that of others. You don't even realize that is the statement you are making when you are late. You're saying, "My time is more valuable than anyone else's." And, that is a negative action that will block success.

At work, there are even more consequences for being late.

**Productivity Loss**

When you're late for work, you create an immediate loss of productivity. If you work as part of a team, your tardiness disrupts the work flow of other team members. If you are late 10 minutes per day, that equals out to almost an hour a week. If a team member needs a late person to provide his or her part of a project, the punctual person still gets behind waiting for what he/she needs from you.

**Negative Morale**

Not only does tardiness make others late, it lowers their morale. If one member of the team doesn't follow the rules, others in that group will began to feel resentment and that the situation is unfair. This is particularly true for those suffering from chronic lateness. It puts stress on others to cover the work of the late employee or fall behind in their own jobs.

### Customer Dissatisfaction

If an employee is late and fails to make an on-time delivery to a customer, the result may be that the business loses that customer. An employee who is supposed to open a specific location at a certain time may lose customers if it isn't opened on time. If the chronic late employee is tardy for customer meetings, this puts the entire company in a bad light. Poor customer service of any type damages a business' reputation and discourages perspective clients.

### Management Problems

If management lets a chronically late employee slide, it creates the potential for loss of respect for those in charge. On-time employees may feel if the rules don't apply then why should they make the effort to be on time! Letting it slide sends the wrong message to the entire company.

### How to Fix it

Everyone slips up and is late occasionally. Traffic, family responsibilities preventing us from getting out the door on time and just everyday life sometimes slow us down. These things happen and sometimes can't be avoided. However, the chronically late person truly has a time-management problem and is totally focused on self instead of the consideration of others. Being late is a product of poor planning. So, here's what you can do to fix it:

- Set your alarm 30 minutes earlier than normal.
- Determine the night before what you will wear the next day and lay it out.
- Don't promise family members that you will handle something "in the morning" when it can be dealt with the night before.
- Plan to be at the office 15 minutes early so you can actually show up on time!

- If traffic is a major factor, plan a new, quicker route, and leave the exact amount of time earlier than you are usually late.
- If getting up 30 minutes earlier still doesn't give you enough time, make it an hour.
- Remember, this is about respecting others and the value of their time. Don't make everything just about you. You will find that others will respect and appreciate you more if you resolve your chronic lateness.

If you are part of a management team that is dealing with chronically late employees, consider sending them to time management coaching, and suggest all of the above! And use the video link[4] in the Video Resources section.

## 18
## How Do You Make Others Feel?

*I've learned that people will forget what you said, people will forget what you did, but people will never forget how you made them feel. –Maya Angelou*

So, how do you make others feel? Do you ask them rude, none-of-your business questions? Do you ignore them when they are speaking to you? Do you criticize their appearance or behavior?

OR do you smile at them, repeat back what they've said to you, help them when they need it, and focus on the positives instead of the negatives?

If you do the latter, then you are a considerate person who makes others feel really good about themselves when they are around you.

### 5 Ways to Make Others around You Feel Great

Dale Partridge of The Daily Positive offers five ways to make the people around you feel great. You might say he is preaching etiquette. I say he's being considerate of others.

- **Put Your Stuff Away** — Don't ever have your phone or computer out while in a conversation.
- **Use a Person's Name in Conversation** — This requires you remember it when they tell you.

- **Ask Them to Teach you Something** — Everyone has something to offer, let them shine.
- **Be Authentically Interested** — Lean in, keep eye contact, and listen way more than you talk.
- **Shine the Spotlight on Them** — In group settings, share someone's talent, a good story about them, or what you like about them.

It's fairly basic behavior, but you would be amazed at how many people don't consider how they make others feel around them. Think about it.

A link to the great Brian Tracy's advice[5] on this subject can be found in the Video Resources section.

# 19
# Four Steps to Overcoming Disappointment

Just as important as how you make others feel, it is critical for you to realize how you make yourself feel. Part of that is how you handle things, like disappointment. I read this remarkable article by Roz Ushcroff that I felt compelled to include in this book.

### Roz Usheroff: Success and Failure

During an interview a few days after a heartbreaking loss at the Super Bowl, Seattle coach Pete Carroll admitted that he awoke in the middle of the night and just wept.

It was a memorable moment in a week of memorable moments, for many reasons.

Besides the admission by a coach from the rough-and-tumble testosterone-filled world of professional football that he had been brought to tears by the setback, one cannot help but wonder about the long-term effect on a championship dynasty if not derailed, then at least delayed.

Of course the determining factor as to whether it is delayed as opposed to being derailed is dependent upon how the team and coaching staff both individually, as well as collectively, react.

When you consider the initial response to what was a huge disappointment on a monumental level, you might be inclined to lean toward the latter. Especially given that many players immediately following the defeat questioned the Seattle Seahawks coach's play calling, while one coach was openly critical of player execution.

This is why Step 1 in the four steps for overcoming disappointment is so critical.

**1. Look Beyond the Immediate Moment**

Winston Churchill once said that "success is not final" and "failure is not fatal," but it is the "courage to continue" that really counts.

While having the courage to go on is without a doubt an attribute, it is the attitude by which you continue that determines future success.

Churchill's "not final-not fatal" perspective speaks to the importance of looking beyond the immediate moment, regardless of whether it is in the bright afterglow of victory or the agony of defeat.

The fact is that even in victory it is important not to let a moment of success define you, because it is in this place of contentment with one's achievement that apathy and a loss of motivation can occur.

Instead, you must use the experience to continue to build toward even greater accomplishments.

The same goes for failure.

In much the same way you should use victory as a springboard for future success, so, too, must you use a setback as a means to achieve a desired outcome.

Ironically, some believe that it is easier to overcome past disappointments than past successes.

Referencing the world of professional sports such as football, this is perhaps one of the reasons why repeat champions are a rarity. Much has been written about the many championship teams that have failed to even qualify for the playoffs, let alone successfully defend their title the year following their big win.

Regardless of one scenario being easier to overcome than the other, one thing is certain ... having the right attitude is the key.

In this context, Carroll's words speak directly to this point when he said; "One moment does not define you; the journey does."

## 2. Accept That Some Things Are Out of Your Control

The wisdom behind recognizing the difference between what you can and cannot change is important.

Sometimes in your life and career, you will do everything that is technically right, but not get the expected result.

To the majority of football fans, Carroll's decision to throw the ball on the doorstep of the opposing team's goal line was unfathomable. But for those who profess to truly understand the game, it was a smart decision that should have but did not work out.

There is no doubt that Carroll's call will forever be debated by everyone who follows professional football. One thing that everyone can agree upon is that the defending player who intercepted the ball made an amazing play.

This, of course, is the unknown variable that turned what appeared to be certain victory into a crushing defeat.

No one could have anticipated the chain of events that led up to that fateful moment, when Malcolm Butler, a little-known first-year player with the New England Patriots, was, at the last minute, sent on the field to defend. He made the play that would catapult him onto the front pages of newspapers around the world, and into gridiron folklore.

There were, of course, other contributing factors at work that in one brief moment conspired to turn the sports world on its ear. If any one of these were removed from the equation, such as New England coach Bill Belichick calling a time out instead of letting the clock run down, there would have likely been a much different outcome.

Once again, contemplating things that never were in an effort to understand what did or did not happen is an exercise in futility. Accept that there will always be factors that are beyond your control and that all you can do is bring your best, whether to the playing field or the boardroom.

### 3. Know When to Let Go of the Past

Amid all of the controversy of what some have referred to as being the worst play call in football history, Carroll's words regarding the importance of the journey demonstrate that there is an intention to let go of the past.

In letting go, I am not suggesting that one forgets the past. After all, what has happened before — good and not so good — has brought you to this present point in your life. It is therefore important to remember and learn from your past experiences so you can continue to build your bigger future.

However, there is a big difference between remembering the past and living in the past.

Like trying to prove or disprove a negative, the futility of which puts you no further ahead than when you started, replaying a past failure over and over again will not change the outcome. The only thing you will accomplish is falling prey to a could-have-would have-should-have mindset that will invariably undermine your future efforts. Instead, you must get beyond what has happened to embrace new opportunities.

### 4. It Is Not What Others Can Live With, But What You Can Live With

In the end, it matters not one iota what others may think in terms of the decisions you make. What does matter is how you feel about your efforts. Can you stand by your choices?

If you can truly look in the mirror and see within yourself someone who did his or her best to deliver the optimum results, then that is what counts.

While there will be many opportunities and outcomes over a lifetime, the values by which you make decisions are the ones that ultimately define you. Remain true to your values and persevere, and you will one day find yourself atop the pinnacle of your hopes and expectations.

### What's More

Do you know the difference between the fear of success and the fear of failure?

Roz Usheroff's guide, *How To Make 2015 Your Breakout Year,* will not only help you to recognize the common obstacles that befall all of us, it will also enable you to take action within the framework of your own unique gifts and abilities to make this year your most successful ever. See the Reference section for a link to her guide.

# 20
## For Women Only ... Not So Much

How you see yourself is critical to your success. It's much more than just how you overcome failure. I discovered some wonderful guidelines through The California Governor & First Lady's Conference on Women, now known as The Women's Conference, the nation's premier forum for women. I've included a video link[6] in the Video Resources Section so you can take a look. Watching the video made it clear to me that the advice to attain success contained within it really is the same for both women and men.

All young women and men can become the architects of change for the future. Highlights from this video provide the following advice to achieve success and make it possible to affect the future in a positive manner. These tips should be taken to heart by every woman, and man.

- Take an idea, believe in it and then surround yourself with talented people who will help you achieve your goals.
- Follow your dreams and your heart. Find your passion. Find what you love and focus on it. Everything will be easier if you do.
- Believe in yourself.
- Don't dismiss your passion — tell everyone about it so the idea will grow ... it is those little

ideas that pop in your head that tell you what you should be doing in your life.

- Don't be afraid to make mistakes. Never be afraid to try. Be authentic, not afraid.
- Listen to your heart and not your head. You do not have to be perfect. Let your intuition lead you. Take risks. Don't hold yourself back.
- Take advantage of opportunities and never give up.
- Be a human being first and foremost. It makes no difference whether you are male or female.
- Both women and men have unique qualities to lead the world. You can be the best thing for your community.
- Speak your mind in meetings. Always be prepared to support your ideas with researched facts.
- Put yourself first for the sake of your health and your wealth.
- Listen to those who came before you. Read the history of other successful people and understand what it takes to push ahead.
- Understand that once you believe you are enough, you can do anything.
- Provoke, inspire, outrage, challenge, dare, imagine, don't blame anyone else for what you do.
- Work hard; there will be judgment from others but focus.
- Find the right mentors ... so many people can be mentors and will be.
- Showing up is the biggest tip to success. If you don't show up, you won't be there to make it happen. Take it seriously!

- Stick to your goals, and don't let others persuade you to do something you don't want to do.

Let this advice guide you to success!

## 21
## How to Be a Friend to a Friend Who's Sick

Let's go back for a heartbeat to how we treat others. Remember, it's the cornerstone to good behavior. Oftentimes we show our true selves when someone else needs us. The worst case scenario for all of us is when a good friend becomes seriously ill.

I have discovered a wonderful little book that covers one of everyone's most dreaded situations. It's entitled *How to Be a Friend to a Friend Who's Sick* by Letty Cottin Pogrebin. She wrote the book because her friends had no idea how to talk to her after her cancer diagnosis in 2009.

Well-intentioned friends often made her feel worse than the disease! Pogrebin's book points out one woman who was diagnosed with cancer eight years after her New York City firefighter husband died at the World Trade Center on 9/11. A friend commented, "Wow! You must have really bad karma! How come you always attract bad luck?" A tasteless, thoughtless comment from someone who had no idea how to comfort her friend.

Pogrebin, a writer, activist and co-founder of *Ms. Magazine*, reiterated how a friend, upon hearing of the author's illness, exclaimed: "Oh, Letty, I was so sad to hear the news! It's almost unbelievable because you've always been so healthful and youthful. How are you?" Pogrebin felt as if her friend was saying, "This is the end of who you are. You will never be young or youthful." It was an erosion of who Pogrebin is as a human being and hurt her deeply.

But Pogrebin soon realized that even though these comments came across badly, it wasn't malice that instigated them but rather lack of knowing what to say. So the author has made it her mission to change the norms of illness etiquette. She took a look at why people struggle so much with what to say and came to the conclusion that it is related to our own vulnerability. When a friend becomes ill, we are reminded of our own mortality. In our culture, illness is very sanitized, says Pogrebin. We don't really talk about what illness looks and feels like and what happens when people don't recover.

Pogrebin suggests that as soon as you learn a person has cancer or another illness, establish conversation that asks:

- Tell me what's helpful and what's not.
- Tell me if you want to be alone and when you want company.
- Tell me what to bring and when to leave.

More than likely, your presence will mean more than sending flowers. Find out what the person really needs, and mean it! Set the tone for really being truthful with each other. Find out if calling a couple of times a week is annoying. Some people, especially Pogrebin, found that emails worked better for her. Some people need a shoulder to cry on and like talking through their illness. Find out what works best for YOUR friend.

### 6 Keys to Helping a Sick Friend

- Ask your sick friend to honestly let you know if he/she wants no visitors or only certain hours of the day.
- Ask "What can I do to help?" instead of "Tell me if you need anything."

- Don't bring food in a dish you want returned. Leave the dish with them or make it your problem to pick it up on the next visit.
- Decide in advance on several topics that might stimulate discussion during your visit. Don't just wing it. Bring a CD, a new app, a movie to watch together or a puzzle to work on with your sick friend.
- Consider helping by cooking a meal, cleaning the house, watering the plants, doing the dishes, walking the dog or changing the sheets.
- Want to give a gift? Try something personal, like a manicure or spa treatment for a female friend or an old-fashioned shave at a barbershop for a male friend.

The greatest gift of all? Pogrebin's daughter, Abigail, summed it up for her. So much of friendship is just being in the room.

I recommend that you grab a copy of this great little book from Amazon.com!

## 22
## Social Media Etiquette for College Students

Speaking of good advice, Leah Polakoff, an outstanding college intern at Pennlive, shared her experiences and great advice for university-bound students. Pennlive kindly granted permission to reprint the article in its entirety. Enjoy!

~ ~ ~

So you're finished high school and are preparing for your first year of college. Take it from a fellow college student, there's a lot of stuff your guidance counselor doesn't prepare you for, like the appropriate ways to use social media in college.

Trust me, there's a world of difference in the Facebook status you post in high school and the ones in college.

### Social Media Etiquette Rule 1

You will join a Facebook group for your graduating class. This is Okay, quite normal actually. These groups are a great way to post questions about classes, events on campus and a way to sell books or used furniture.

What's not normal is going through the entire list and adding every single person in the group that you haven't met. Unless you have a specific reason for adding them, try to

69

refrain. It's weird and borderline stalker-ish. Please, just don't do it.

And if someone de-friends you, they probably did it for a reason. Don't overreact to this by sending them multiple messages and adding them back. The damage has already been done.

### Social Media Etiquette Rule 2

Within these college Facebook groups, your dorm's resident assistant (known simply as your "RA") might make a group solely for your floor.

Here it's Okay to add everyone; these groups are made as a way for you to get to know everybody. Post activities you'd like to do with people from your floor, ask questions about the ring you lost in the bathroom and see if anybody wants to go to the dining hall with you.

But when posting pictures on your own page, make sure you have current ones. You're going to meet tons (and I mean tons) of new people in the first couple of weeks. If you've recently dyed your hair brown, but you're blonde in all of your Facebook pictures, people on your floor might not recognize you. You don't want to be known as that girl on the fifth floor who looks better on Facebook. It makes things awkward.

### Social Media Etiquette Rule 3

To all your high school friends back home, you're basically the coolest kid on the planet. I mean, you're in college now! But to all the upperclassmen at your university, you're just a freshman. We've all been there, done that.

Please refrain from Tweeting and Instagram-ing every little thing about the college campus. We all know the dining hall food sucks, there are a billion squirrels on campus and using the #college after everything is annoying.

### Social Media Etiquette Rule 4

Not all of your professors are going to be old and boring. Especially at big schools, you'll most likely be taking classes taught by graduate students (which is just as awesome as it sounds). They tend to be a lot cooler and more laid back than professors who are tenured. But no matter how cool your graduate student teacher is, do not add them on Facebook or follow them on Twitter until the class is over. I repeat, do not connect with your teachers via social media until the semester ends and you're sure you won't have any more classes with them. Let's be real, if you skip that 8 a.m. class on Friday morning do you really want them to see your party pics on Facebook from Thursday night?

### Social Media Etiquette Rule 5

And speaking of those party pics from Rule 4, just go back and delete those. I'll probably sound like a broken record of your parents, but refrain from posting pictures of you out drinking, smoking cigarettes or at parties. It doesn't matter how many private settings you have on your Twitter, Instagram or Facebook. If a future employer wants to hack into your page, they will find a way.

You're in college to get an education and ultimately find a job. Nobody will take your internship application seriously if your profile picture involves a red Solo cup and beer bong. Un-tag and avoid posting photos that involve partying. Do a quick Google search of your name just to double check nothing embarrassing comes up.

This doesn't mean you have to run from a camera when you're out. Just be smart about what pictures go online and what pictures are simply for your own entertainment.

## 23
## How to Get Around Town, with Courtesy

What about behavior when you are out and about? When you are going to and from work; headed for lunch; doing your shopping or just generally enjoying the outdoors, it's easy to forget the "little things" that show appreciation for others and make everyone's life easier. Call them "common courtesies" if you will, but if they were "common" we wouldn't forget to do them!

Journey with me through some points to remember.

- Walk in the same direction as traffic on the sidewalk. If you are approaching someone, pass them on your right (their left).
- Men, if you are with a female, walk[7] on the outside of the sidewalk. Why? It's a common courtesy that began in England at least as far back as the time of Shakespeare. Originally, it was to protect women from the possibility of being run over or splashed with mud by carriages. In addition, because people threw their trash out the windows onto the street, women were shielded by men to prevent them from getting covered in garbage or worse! A man also walked on the right to leave his sword arms free and to have space to use it. The sword

72

was worn on the man's left but unsheathed with the right hand. While we don't have to contend with swordplay or mud and garbage from the streets, today it is considered a "gentlemanly" and polite courtesy.

- Skateboarders and bicyclists should never ride on the sidewalk, only in the bike lanes. It is dangerous to do so among pedestrians.
- Avoid jaywalking. Primarily, it is dangerous to your health and that of others. Go to a crosswalk and stop. Make sure both the car nearest you and those behind it see you and stop. You don't want the car stopping for you at a crosswalk to get rear-ended.
- If you see a blind or elderly person needing help at a crosswalk, approach that person on the left and let him or her know you would like to help. Take the person's left arm and help him or her across, indicating when to step up or down. That person will appreciate your kindness, and it will make you feel better about yourself as well.
- Open doors for people with canes, wheelchairs or scooters for the disabled. Look at and speak to them. Don't look away or avoid eye contact. Doing so is hurtful to them and makes them feel they don't exist. While you are at it, open doors for both men and women, whether they are elderly or not. It's just the polite thing to do.
- Use the 10-5-3 Rule as you approach people. When you are 10 feet away, acknowledge the person with your eyes. When you are 5 feet away, smile and nod your head. When you are 3 feet away, greet the person with "hello." Not everyone will do so, but it is a great way to brighten someone else's day. Think about it.

73

When you are acknowledged, doesn't it lighten your step a bit?

- Don't text while walking[7] (or driving, for that matter.) If you need to text, step to the side, stop and do so. Otherwise, you will run into others or into a solid object or open hole that might send you to the hospital. When you are talking on the phone, be aware of where you're going and don't walk out into the street or otherwise put yourself in harm's way.
- On a moving sidewalk or escalator, always stay to the right to make it easy for others to pass you on the left. In other words, don't block the passing lane. The same goes when you are driving. Stay out of the passing lane unless you are going around another car.
- When the elevator doors open, let those on it unload before you board. Young boys and men should hold the doors open for others. Again, it is just another common courtesy.
- When driving and two cars are at a stop sign, the car on the right has the right-of-way. It is the law and is courteous. Don't cut off other cars or use your vehicle as a way to take out your general frustrations. It is an act of hostility that can end a life — yours or another.
- Finally, use your car horn only as a safety factor, not to impatiently urge others through a light or turn. You may not be able to see that they are waiting for a pedestrian or another car to pass.

Some will say that this is an outdated way to behave. My response? Since when are good manners, kindness, consideration for others and courtesy outdated?

## 24
## How to Say "No" to Donation Requests

If you work in an office, are a parent or just plain have friends, you've most often been tapped to "donate to a worthy cause." Not once, or twice, but multiple times on a regular basis. I don't know about you, but I literally cringe when I have to disappoint someone who asks for my help. That's all part of me trying to be considerate of others.

First of all, I am in no way suggesting that you should not give to charity. We all should give when we can to support others. But the operative words are "when we can." And, if you are like me, when "we can't" because money is tight or you just aren't inclined to do so, you feel terrible. You may not always know what to say in those situations.

Because I never like to let anyone down, I read with interest Julie Blais Comeau's article, "Sticky Situations: Saying No to Charity: in *The Huffington Post Canada.* She offered the following guidelines that I felt were helpful.

- In times like this, and actually at all times, you should respect yourself and be true to your budget foremost. Set your own limits. Make them annual, seasonal, or monthly, as you wish.
- Define your charitable objectives and have a clear set of giving rules. Pick a charity of

choice or make a prioritized list of favorites. This way, when you allocate within your budget, you will have a personal code of giving for the causes that you identify and empathize with. Should your financial situation change, you will be able to refer back to your objectives and adjust accordingly.

- Remember, it is always appropriate to say that you have an annual charity budget and that you have already allocated it to your charity of choice. Businesses do this all the time. Use the same principle for your donations.

- You may add that you would be happy to consider them next year. If you so wish, you may even want to ask to be reminded in advance.

- You can always offer to contribute your talents and your time, in lieu of money.

- Honesty also works. When, and if you ever choose to go that route, in the case of a charity that you had supported for many years and simply cannot afford to or do not wish to donate this year, simply say: "I really believe in your cause and was always proud to support it. Unfortunately, this year I will have to decline but, I do hope to continue to support it next year."

- Don't feel guilty. Philanthropic giving is a personal choice, so no guilt should be associated when declining to give.

In addition, if you find that you are being asked at work to the point that you are beginning to feel uncomfortable, and you are going through tough times financially, Comeau suggests you speak to HR and inform them privately of your situation. They may be aware of similar situations within your team and may, as a result, implement a "No solicitation at work" policy.

Remember, you do have a choice to give, to go to a fundraiser or to participate, or not. Just because you are asked does not mean you must say yes. HOWEVER, if you are invited to a fundraiser or an event of any kind that sends an RSVP and you can't or do not wish to attend, don't just throw the invite in the trash. RESPOND! Please do not display bad behavior just because you do not want to attend.

The point of these suggestions is to set up honest objectives to accommodate charitable giving while supporting the causes closest to your heart. In that way, you can continue to help others and not feel badly about not being able to always support everyone. See the supporting video[8] in the Video Resources section.

# 25
# Love Is Not Abuse

What does that have to do with behavior?

Abuse is an unacceptable behavior, and it is imperative that all of us put forth the effort to break the cycle of abuse when we see it. Not all but some abused become abusers. That is a cycle that our society should never tolerate.

Everyone deserves respect. And, in a relationship, each partner should be an equal. Physical, mental or emotional abuse, including neglect, should never come into play in any relationship.

I was shocked to learn that, according to a 2010 national survey, more men than women were victims of Intimate partner physical violence. That's right, more than 40 percent of severe physical violence was directed at men. And, men are more often the victim of psychological aggression.

Statistics also reveal that one in every four women will experience domestic violence in her lifetime. An estimated 1.3 million women are victims of physical assault by an intimate partner each year. And, historically, females have been most often victimized by someone they knew.

Females who are 20-24 years of age are at the greatest risk of nonfatal intimate partner violence. Even with these horrific statistics, the capper is that most cases of domestic violence are never reported to the police.

**Physical Abuse**

I teach my students that it is never Okay to hit another person. It is never Okay to allow another person to physically abuse you, and that it is always the person who does the abusing who is to blame. Why? Because most people who are abused believe that they deserve this type of treatment.

**Mental Abuse**
- Mental abuse comes in a variety of forms:
- Yelling (which is never a proper response)
- Giving the silent treatment (emotional and mental abuse) or neglect
- Demoralizing another for his or her beliefs or actions (which is NEVER acceptable). It is important for us to honor the decisions that our friends and family make.

**Breaking the Abuse Cycle**

The key to breaking the abuse cycle is "awareness." The more that it is written and talked about, the more aware those suffering from abuse will become. Those who are abused or live in a home where abuse occurs need to discover that:
- Love does not include abuse.
- If you have seen this at home, it does not make it acceptable.
- Abuse is not a cultural thing.
- Parents should never let their children think it is Okay.
- Abuse is wrong no matter WHAT!

**For an Abused Person Reading This:**

A friend of mine was the victim of physical, mental and emotional abuse for more than a decade. She wrote out some advice she thought might be helpful from one who overcame an abusive relationship. This is what she offers:

- Know that you are a worthy human being. Stop living in the past. Those who do are still hiding behind past events and think they aren't worthy of better than they have.
- Surround yourself with winners. Associate with those who make you feel positive about yourself, who help you believe that you "can if you think you can!"
- Don't let anyone else rule your destiny. Take control of your life.
- Label yourself as STRONG, not weak. Believe in that strength. Know that you can do anything you set your heart and mind to do.
- Take responsibility for your past and current mistakes, and then leave them behind you like the useless baggage they are. Don't blame anyone else for your past ... it's all you, baby.
- Stop living in a "poor little me" pity party. Get out of the doldrums and focus on what you want out of life.
- If you are like I was, stop always choosing the "easy way out," which is sometimes the "do nothing" route. The easy road is rarely the right road. The bottom line? It's all about attitude. You may not change the situation, but you can change your attitude about any and everything. When you do that, your situation will change. Here is a list of Resources:

How to Help Someone Who Is Being Abused
http://www.emergecenter.org/get-help/how-to-help-someone-who-is-being-abused/

How to Help a Friend Who Is Being Abused
https://www.womenshealth.gov/violence-against-women/get-help-for-violence/how-to-help-a-friend-who-is-being-abused.html

Help a Loved One or Friend
http://abuseintervention.org/help/friend-family/

Recognizing, Preventing and Reporting Child Abuse
http://www.helpguide.org/articles/abuse/child-abuse-and-neglect.htm

# WORKPLACE CONDUCT

# Why Workplace Conduct Matters

Having worked on the fringe of corporate life most of my career in the event business, I was always shocked, amused and amazed with the discrepancies in business decorum displayed by different industries. Yes each and every sector of business seems to have a different code of etiquette or proper behavior. For instance, in the entrepreneurial world, things are far more relaxed as far as dress code is concerned. However, the work hours may be far longer than those experienced in the corporate arena.

Everyone involved in small startups tend to emphasize team work with the primary goal of making the business a success. This is much more evident in the small business model simply because people are more in tune with the finances in smaller companies. Team work is essential here because everyone needs mutual cooperation with a smaller staff, and team members need to rely heavily on each other. Unfortunately, this isn't always the case in larger companies.

Larger companies tend to emphasize important rules and a strict code of proper, professional behavior. This is essential when a large number of people come together in the work place. This reaches from dress code to how you should get your boss' attention. In a larger company, employees will often go to the HR department with problems. In smaller companies, HR departments most likely don't exist. So, concerns or challenges would be brought to an immediate supervisor.

But, whether you work in a small or large business, each of us needs to fit into the culture of the organization. Yes the rules may be different; however, it's on you to be able to get along with your business associates.

If you are part of a team, even in a vendor-client relationship, the behavior you use to develop long-term synergy is imperative. For instance, during my career in the event industry as a designer, Gillette was one of my long-time clients. Back in the 1990s, they were the major sponsor for the World Cup being held in Los Angeles. For one of the galas, I had given them an idea they loved for table centerpieces, but it was too extravagant for the budget. So, rather than letting me go back and research further, they asked me for a new idea on the spot. We had the type of camaraderie that allowed for us to trust each other. Thinking out loud, I came up with an idea to put a soccer ball, a shoe and a helmet on sod in the middle of the table. My client team members looked at me like I'd lost my mind.

The client lead calmly smiled and said, "John, soccer players don't wear helmets."

They most likely would have fired anyone else who didn't have the history we had together! Imagine making that kind of mistake with a client! But I had never even seen a soccer game. My bad. So, instead of firing me, they took my wife Marti and me to the semi-finals at the Rose Bowl in prime center seats practically on the field. When one of the teams scored, 1,000 doves were released. And low and behold, one flew straight to me and landed in my hands! A photo of that ended up on the front page of the sports section of the *Los Angeles Times.* When that appeared, I told my client, "I may not know soccer, but I sure can get you PR!"

Because of all the relationship building combined with my ongoing considerate behavior toward my client and the use of the tools in this section, Gillette forgave my error. One, by the way, I never committed again. I always did my homework after that!

I hope within this next section you will find the help needed to perfect relationships with others, as well as yourself, in the work place. These are all tried and true tools. Enjoy!

# 26
# What Employers REALLY Want

Wish you knew how to win the hearts and minds of current or perspective employers? Want to make them beam at the thought of making you a part of their team or hand you that next big promotion?

Every employer seeks unique skills that match a particular job. But they also seek out "universal skills" or "soft skills." If you don't have these "soft skills," you can definitely gain them with training or coaching and mentoring from someone who understands them. Once you've got them, you can tailor your job search résumés, cover letters or interview language to highlight them.

What are these magical "employable skills"? I went on a search for them and found them in a list that Drs. Randall S. and Katharine Hansen compiled. The list was culled from a number of recent studies. While I haven't included all of them, I've listed what I feel are the criticals.

### Critical Skills Employers Seek
- **Listening, Verbal and Written Communications.** A communicator who actually listens and then conveys the information effectively both verbally and in writing.

- **Analytical/Research Skills.** Your ability to assess a situation, seek multiple perspectives, gather more information if necessary, and identify key issues that need to be addressed. On a résumé, you'd want to stress you possess highly analytical thinking and talent for identifying, scrutinizing, improving and streamlining complex work processes.

- **Computer/Technical Literacy.** Almost all jobs now require basic understanding of word processing, spreadsheets and email. Let the employer know you are computer-literate on a wide variety of apps.

- **Flexibility/Adaptability/Managing Multiple Priorities.** Show you can multitask, adapt to changing work assignments and prioritize. Stress you are a flexible team player who thrives on juggling simultaneous projects.

- **The ability to relate to your co-workers, inspire others to participate, and mitigate conflict.** Indicate you are a relationship-builder with highly effective interpersonal skills.

- **Multicultural Sensitivity/Awareness.** Diversity is the biggest issue in the workplace. Workers who illustrate a sensitivity and awareness to other people and cultures are prized. State flat-out that cultural sensitivity and building rapport with a diverse workforce in a multicultural environment is a strength.

- **Planning/Organizing.** Ultra important. Means you can design, plan, organize and coordinate projects with deadlines. It also means you know how to set goals and achieve them. Play up the importance of your planning and organizational skills and detail orientation.

- **Problem-Solving/Reasoning/Creativity.** The ability to find solutions to problems using your creativity, reasoning and past experiences along with the available information and resources. State that you are a problem-solver who can provide solutions and resolve issues.
- **Teamwork.** The aptitude to work with others professionally to achieve a common goal. Make a point to illustrate you can build trust with colleagues and customers.

Wondering where you stand on some of the most sought-after soft skills? Use the URL to the Employability Skills Assessmenta, prepared by Dr. Randall S. Hansen, also found in the Reference Section.

# 27
## Personal Values Employers Want in Employees

After looking at the critical skills employers seek, let's examine the personal values employers want in employees. Again, I draw upon lists compiled by Drs. Randall S. and Katharine Hansen from numerous studies.

Values, personality traits and personal characteristics are just as important as skills to employers. When writing résumés, cover letters and answering interview questions, look for ways to weave examples of these characteristics into them.

Here is the Hansen List of the 10 most important categories of values.

- **Honesty/Integrity/Morality.** In light of the many corporate scandals, employers probably respect personal integrity more than any other value. So emphasize that you are a seasoned pro whose honesty and integrity support effective leadership and optimize business relationships.

- **Adaptability/Flexibility.** Show that you are open to new concepts and ideas and can work either independently or as part of a team. Stress that you are capable of handling multiple tasks or projects. Use words like highly adaptable, positive, resilient, mobile, patient risk-taker open to new ideas.

- **Dedication/Hard-Working/Work Ethic/Tenacity.** Employers want job-seekers who love what they do and will stick with it until they solve the problem and get the job done. Use words like: I am a productive worker with a solid work ethic who maximizes my effort to successfully complete tasks.
- **Dependability/Reliability/Responsibility.** These are extremely important to employers. They want to know that they can count on you to show up on time and take responsibility for your actions. Emphasize that you are a dependable, responsible contributor committed to success and excellence.
- **Loyalty.** Even when the company is not necessarily loyal to its employees, employers want workers who will have a strong devotion to the company. Include words on your résumé or in conversation, such as I am a loyal and dedicated manager with an excellent work record.
- **Positive/Motivated/Passionate/Energetic.** The job-seekers who get hired and the employees who get promoted are the ones with drive and passion — and who demonstrate this enthusiasm through their words and actions. Use words that convey you are an energetic performer with a passion for work. Show that you have a positive, upbeat attitude.
- **Professionalism.** Show that you act in a responsible and fair manner in both your personal and work life. This is a sign of maturity and self-confidence; avoid being petty. You can illustrate that you are a

conscientious go-getter who is dedicated, organized and committed to professionalism.

- **Self-Confidence.** If you believe in yourself, in your unique mix of skills, education and abilities, your prospective employer will also feel the same. Show confidence in what you can offer employers. State outright that you are a confident, hard-working employee committed to excellence.

- **Self-Motivated/Independent Worker Needing Little or No Supervision.** Teamwork is always important to employers as is the ability to work independently, with minimal supervision. Tell the prospective employer that you are a highly motivated self-starter who takes initiative with little supervision.

- **Willingness to Learn.** No matter what your age, no matter how much experience you have, you should always be willing to learn a new skill or technique. Jobs are constantly changing and evolving, and you must show an openness to grow and learn with that change. Say that you are an enthusiastic, knowledge-hungry learner, eager to meet challenges and assimilate new concepts.

While your skills are critical tools, don't forget that your personal values are necessary to your success at work. Once you have assessed the necessary skills and values you need to win a job or advance in it, don't forget to document them and market yourself, in both your job search (résumé, cover letter and interview answers) and during your efforts for career advancement. Learn more about how to match your personal qualities to the job[9] by following the video link in the Video Resources Section.

# 28
# 9 Meeting Rules for Pros

Want to be considered a "meeting pro?" Follow these 9 rules to make the grade.

**1. Don't be late.**

That's right; everyone else's time is just as important as yours. So if you're running a meeting with multiple participants, start the meeting on time. Late comers will just have to catch up, and maybe next meeting be on time. If you are in a client-vendor situation, and you are the vendor, then obviously hold the meeting for the client. Unfortunately, most clients feel their time is more valuable than yours, and if you want the business, you'll need to be aware that's how the cookie crumbles.

**2. Call ahead if you are going to be late.**

Everyone knows that, right? Wrong. They might know it, but they don't adhere to it. I can't count the number of times that I've sat waiting on someone to show up for an appointment in my office, or waited in their office for them to see me. Allow enough time before scheduled meetings to show up at the appointed hour.

**3. Dress appropriately.**

If you are going to meet a client or another associate at his/her office, find out what the general dress code is for that business. This is particularly important the first time you meet with someone. When I was just starting out, I NEVER wore a suit. However, I had the chance to make a presentation to Delta Airlines. I researched and discovered they wore suits to work. So, I followed suit, so to speak. Halfway through the presentation, I asked if I might remove my jacket as the room was quite warm. Everyone removed their jackets! And guess what, I got the business. It wasn't so much that I just wore a suit, but I wouldn't have been credible to them walking in the door if I hadn't.

In the case of an all-day meeting, the facilitator should provide information regarding the preferred dress code, whether it is causal or formal.

**4. Provide an agenda if you are chairing the meeting.**

The agenda should be circulated in advance with as much lead time as appropriate. Participants should provide any issues or changes with topics at least 24-hours in advance.

**5. Do not put your cell phone on the table during a meeting.**

If you use an iPad to take notes, let your host or facilitator know that you are using your iPad for that purpose. Otherwise, everyone will think you are busy working on what you consider to be "more important" issues. Don't take calls during a meeting. If you are expecting an urgent call, let the host or facilitator know that you have unavoidable issues that might require you to take an important call or text. Once the call comes through, excuse yourself, get up and go out of the room to a private area where you won't disturb others. I'll never forget an important meeting with a client where one of my associates got a call, held up her finger, answered the call and then went into the hall. She didn't shut the door and instead had a loud and quite emotional conversation with the party on the other end of the phone. I was embarrassed beyond belief, and guess what, we didn't get the business!

**6. Don't interrupt someone when he or she is speaking.**

Oftentimes meeting participants become so enthusiastic about the issues at hand that they forget their manners. We've all done it. That doesn't mean you have to raise your hand to speak, but a slight gesture to indicate you have something to add as soon as the previous person has completed his/her input works. And never have "side conversations" while others are talking. Try to treat others with the respect you would like to receive.

**7. If you are attending a meeting, be prepared.**

A meeting can be derailed quickly if you fail to bring the necessary materials for the meeting. Think that's a no-brainer? Think again. I've scrapped plenty of meetings because participants didn't bring the necessary materials.

**8. Avoid nervous habits.**

Don't tap your pen or pencil on the table. Don't make audible noises with your mouth, roll your eyes in disagreement or disrespect, tap your feet on the floor or rustle your papers. I once had a colleague who incessantly sighed during meetings. It was never clear whether he was frustrated, tired or bored!

**9. Be attentive and respectful.**

Don't stare at your fingernails. Look at others while they are speaking and be prepared to add constructive solutions. Don't argue or try one-upmanship during a meeting. If you do disagree, politely provide alternative solutions. Don't try to embarrass anyone but rather offer the alternatives in a professional manner. I once was in a meeting with approximately 20 other people, and the chairman of the meeting purposely embarrassed one of the female professionals by insulting her. Everyone was stunned into momentary silence, and then yours truly asked him to apologize and set a more professional tone for the meeting. Everyone voiced his/her opinion from around the room to support my comments. The man was a lost cause, but at least everyone else in the meeting felt good about defending our colleague.

See "How to Practice Proper Business Meeting Etiquette"[10] in the Video Resources Section.

# 29
# How to Avoid Lapses in Workplace Ethics

The best way to shoot holes in your self-image is to create lapses in workplace ethics. This will destroy your chances for advancement and have coworkers distancing themselves from you.

So, what are fundamental workplace ethics? Do you make up excuses for your behavior? Do you feel guilty after you've failed to act ethically on any given circumstance? Susan M. Heathfield — author of an article "Did You Bring Your Ethics to Work Today?" — lists examples of employees failing to practice fundamental workplace ethics.

- You take office supplies from work to use at home because you justify that you often engage in company work at home, or you worked extra hours this week, etc.
- You use the last roll of toilet paper or the last piece of paper towel in the company restroom. Without thought for the needs of the next employee, you go back to work rather than addressing the issue.
- You call in sick to your supervisor because it's a beautiful day to go to the beach, or shopping, or ...

97

- You engage in an affair with a coworker while married because no one at work will ever know. You think you're in love; you think you can get away with it; your personal matters are your own business; the affair will not have an impact on other employees or the workplace, yada, yada, yada ... Right.
- You place your dirty cup in the lunchroom sink. With a guilty glance around the room, you find no one watching and quickly leave.
- Your company sponsors events, activities or lunches and you sign up to attend and fail to show. Conversely, you fail to sign up and show up anyway. You make the behavior worse when you say that you took the appropriate action so someone else must have screwed up.
- You tell potential customers that you are the vice president in charge of something. When they seek out the company VP at a trade show, you tell your boss that the customers must have made a mistake.
- You work in a restaurant in which wait staff tips are shared equally and you withhold a portion of your tips from the common pot before the tips are divided.
- You have sex with a reporting staff member and then provide special treatment to your flame. How about you just have sex, period? No impact? Wrong! Can you spell sexual harassment?
- You spend several hours a day using your work computer to shop, check out sports scores, pay bills, do online banking, and surf the headlines for the latest celebrity news and political opinions.

- You use up the last paper in the communal printer and you fail to replace paper, leaving the task to the next employee who uses the printer.
- You hoard supplies in your desk drawer so you won't run out while other employees go without supplies they need to do their work.
- You overhear a piece of juicy gossip about another employee and then repeat it to coworkers. Whether the gossip is true is not the issue. Trust me.
- You tell a customer or potential customer that your product will perform a particular action when you don't know if it will and you don't check with an employee who does.
- You allow a part that you know does not meet quality standards leave your work station and hope your supervisor or the quality inspector won't notice.
- You claim credit for the work of another employee, or you fail to give public credit to a coworker's contribution, when you share results, make a presentation, turn in a report or in any other way appear to be the sole owner of a work product or results.
- You fudge your expense account, claiming more expenses and falsifying receipts spent on personal rather than business use or misuse company assets.
- You have a close personal relationship with a contractor that constitutes a conflict of interest.

This is by no means a comprehensive list of workplace ethical failures. You will be able to get away with some of them. The rest will catch up to you. This type of behavior is addictive and grows. After the first time, it becomes easier and easier.

The point is that without ethics, there is no trust, no respect and certainly no real chance for this type of behavior to propel you into success. Like lies, unethical behavior will catch up with you eventually and destroy everything that you've tried to build.

Think about all the other types of unethical behaviors that are possible and avoid them like they are the plague. If you've behaved unethically in the past, change your behavior to protect your future.

Check out the video link[11] on Unethical Behavior in the Video Resources Section.

## 30
## Building a House of Cards with Unethical Behavior

I have to admit that Netflix's *House of Cards* is a fascinating study of unethical behavior that leads to corruption. Frank Underwood's need for revenge and lack of ethics clearly have paved the way for his criminal behavior. And, I have to admit that the series has fascinated me with its clear purpose of showing the path to destruction. As pointed out above, unethical behavior can easily become a part of an individual's modus operandi.

I read with interest Amy Rees Anderson's article on passive-aggressive behavior in *Forbes* magazine, and frankly couldn't see a difference between what she described and unethical behavior. Anderson's description of passive aggression mirrors Underwood's unethical behavior.

- On the surface, the person appears to be agreeable and supportive, but behind the scenes will backstab, undercut and sabotage.
- This person constantly states that you can trust his words when his actions have consistently shown that not to be true.
- He makes promises about things when he has no intention of ever following through, often then blaming things that were "out of his

control" for precluding him from being able to fulfill his promise.

- He states "I was supportive of you, but this other person wasn't so there is nothing I can do" in order to place blame on someone else rather than voicing his own lack of support for the matter.
- He gives positive praise and feedback to you directly, but then takes actions to undercut you to coworkers and management.
- He withholds important information from other employees to make himself appear more important and more valuable and in an attempt to make others around him fail.
- He uses sarcasm or humor to make fun of someone else so he can hide behind an "I was just kidding" attitude, when really he meant every word.
- Finally, he wants everyone to believe that he is their biggest supporter and advocate, refusing to be honest and direct with his true feelings.

If you are an employee dealing with a manager operating in this manner, bring it to the attention of the chief executive officer. This unethical manager has an agenda, and it's not one that will be kind to you. Don't stand by and let it happen. This is a risk for you, but putting your career in the hands of someone you can't trust is even worse.

If you are honest and respectful in the manner in which you voice your concerns, your thoughts will be welcomed. If you are working under a management that promotes this type of behavior, leave it behind and find a company culture filled with respect and integrity.

For more information, use the video link in the Resources section entitled: What Makes Unethical Behavior Contagious?[12]

# 31
# Unprofessional Behavior Could Lose Business and Your Job!

Times are changing. Social norms have varied in today's world but that doesn't mean basic etiquette doesn't matter. Take Brad Smith, for instance. His company had high hopes for what they thought would be a young mover and shaker. Brad was filled with self-confidence and felt fairly invincible out of the gate. But he forgot that business is really about people and that most of us would rather work with or buy from someone with professional behavior and high standards.

Brad was good about introducing people, but he often substituted a "hello" or nod **instead of offering a handshake**. When he was busy, he **often failed to acknowledge or greet his co-workers** unless he needed something from them. His management began to notice and thought it displayed that he was unapproachable and impolite. Their suspicions were backed up when he **failed to say "please" or "thank you"** for anything.

Brad was an "over-talker." He was so eager to impress his own opinions that he **often interrupted others** in midsentence. It's never easy to not interject, particularly when there is a point to be made. But Brad always pressed on, rudely disrespecting the opinions of others. He often appeared

103

aggressive rather than assertive. In the heat of conversation, he sometimes used **derogatory, rude or offensive language**. His **written communications were filled with slang**, which added to the unprofessional impression he began to make on others. Oftentimes he would **send emails without subject lines and content full of spelling and grammar errors**. Instead of a proper closure, he would sign his emails with a smiley face!

After a few months on the job, Brad got in the **habit of walking into someone's office unannounced**. No knock on the door or hello before opening it. Never questioning if it was a good time to talk. He never called or emailed ahead to find a good time to talk. His direct supervisors felt disrespected and often spoke to Brad about calling ahead. But Brad just ignored his boss' words of warning. Brad also liked **to stand over the boss' shoulder at his desk and read over his shoulder or hang around and listen** as his supervisor finished a phone call.

Brad developed a reputation among his co-workers as a **gossip who liked to bait others on highly charged topics of politics and religion and then share those discussions to irritate others**. He crossed the personal and professional lines on this one.

In meetings, (for which he was **frequently late**) whether in-house or with clients, he would **stop the conversation to take calls, or he would text or check emails**. He **failed to show genuine interest through eye contact and making an effort to truly listen to others**. He was easily distracted and began to lose business. Management began to lose patience and started writing him up because of his behavior.

After three warnings in six months, the company let him go. Is it any wonder that it took them so long?

As you go about your professional career, remember that companies hire for aptitude and work knowledge but often fire for behavior. It is something to always keep in mind.

## 32
## Attitude vs. Aptitude and Hiring for a
## Company Culture Fit

When I wrote the last paragraph of the previous article, I was reminded of a *60 Minutes* segment entitled "Years Up" that I watched more than a year ago. It focused on an organization helping youth to get internships. It is very much on target with The Key Class. What struck me in this piece was this group's emphasis on "hiring for skills and firing for behavior."

A week or so later, I read with interest a guest blog for Extraordinary Events, written by my long-time friend, Bonnie Siegel, the founder and CEO of ASE Group, an event production firm based in Overland Park, Kansas. In it, Siegel takes a slightly different approach to hiring the best and the brightest.

"My approach is to hire for Culture Fit," she explained. "I don't care as much about from what school they graduated or where they worked in the past. We have somewhat perfected an in-house process that tests whether they will fit in with our culture. If they fit, they can be trained to give the 'ASE Experience' to a client. I can't train or mentor or teach our culture. They are either 'wired' to fit in or not."

This holds value for me. It goes to the "hire for attitude; train for aptitude" theory that has been growing among business.

Bill Taylor, the co-founder of *Fast Company*, points out in an article from the *Harvard Business Review:* Arkadi Kuhlmann, founder and CEO of ING Direct USA, has invented a whole new approach to retail banking. Over the past decade, as he has recruited thousands of employees to his organization, he has made it a point not to look to his competitors as a source of talent.

"If you want to renew and re-energize an industry," he told Taylor, "don't hire people from that industry. You've got to untrain them and then retrain them. I'd rather hire a jazz musician, a dancer, or a captain in the Israeli Army. They can learn about banking. It's much harder for bankers to unlearn their bad habits."

Taylor goes on to say that "the game-changers at Southwest Airlines" that constantly challenges conventional wisdom in that business "have embraced the hire for attitude philosophy more intensely than any big organization."

Sherry Phelps a 33-year top exec at Southwest explained the philosophy to Taylor.

"The first thing we look for is the 'warrior spirit'," Phelps said. "So much of our history was born out of battles — fighting for the right to be an airline, fighting off the big guys who wanted to squash us, now fighting off the low-cost airlines trying to emulate us. We are battle-born, battle-tried people. Anyone we add has to have some of that warrior spirit."

This all makes sense because when you hire for cultural fit you end up with a more cohesive workforce, and it improves engagement and retention rates. However, I decided to take a closer look.

Raj Sheth, co-founder of Recruiterbox, an online recruitment and applicant tracking system, suggests hiring for both attitude and aptitude. In a piece for ere.net, he says:

"There has recently been such a strong push to hire for attitude that skills are steadily falling by the wayside. Job Preparedness Indicator research from the Career Advisory Board, established by DeVry University, found that only 17 percent of 516 hiring managers said that job seekers have the skills and traits their organizations are looking for in a candidate."

Sheth goes on to say that LeadershipIQ performed a three-year study of 5,247 hiring managers and tracked 20,000 new hires; 46 percent of them failed within 18 months. But even more surprising than the failure rate was that when new hires failed, 89 percent of the time it was for attitudinal reasons and only 11 percent of the time for a lack of skill. Bad attitudes or attitudes that aren't in line with the company culture will lead to high turnover. High turnover then leads to low morale, upset productivity and high talent acquisitions costs."

Hiring managers who still emphasize aptitude are reviewing their top employees and trying to locate candidates like them, says Sheth. So they suggest identifying top talent, charting their values, skills, communication type, etc. and targeting sourcing, interviewing and hiring processes to reach those people. In his recommendation, Sheth quotes HR pro John Myrna, "Hire based on aptitude, i.e. having enough gray matter to master the skills, and attitude, i.e. the passion and commitment to put in the time to master the skills."

Interesting food for thought, don't you think?

For more input, follow the link for the video on "Do Managers Hire for Attitude or Aptitude?"[13] in the Video Resources Section.

# 33
# Why Gossip in the Workplace is Lethal

I've been focusing on hiring for attitude, so let's take a moment to examine some bad attitude coupled with unacceptable behavior. One example is gossip. Maybe you think that gossip is a harmless, unavoidable element of the workplace. It isn't. Left unchecked, gossip wreaks havoc on company morale and efficiency.

That doesn't mean that you can't discuss who had drinks together after work. I'm referring to talk among coworkers, managers and executives about work-related matters to someone who can't do anything about it. When you don't discuss this with someone who can help the situation, you are not being upfront and honest. Rather, you are being a coward.

Unfortunately, most human beings are prone to complaining. Most often it is not productive and results in resentment that blocks collaboration and good communication.

This doesn't mean you should never voice a negative opinion about anything work-related. It should never discourage you from questioning anything. However, most workplace gossip is often about issues that truly concern the company and should be openly discussed with management. These include:

- Company layoffs
- Why budgets are cut from one department and not another
- The boss taking sole credit for another individual or team member's work

These things are toxic for the entire company. An organization that is free of gossip provides a place for honest communications. Employers are able to deal with issues upfront and address them to the individual who can actually do something about them. This enhances teamwork, trust and good communication.

### The Keys to Preventing Gossip

- Management must declare that work is a no-gossip zone.
- To avoid engaging in gossip, steer clear of places where gossip abounds (like the coffee pot) or where people who are likely to partake in it linger. If others start gossiping, change the subject. If the gossiper doesn't take the hint, tell him or her directly that you would prefer not to gossip. Or excuse yourself to handle some legitimate business activity.
- Information among coworkers often gets misinterpreted or exaggerated. That results in spreading rumors. Eventually, your manager will hear the gossip and get a distorted version of your concerns rather than what you truly meant or said. Don't repeat gossip from others. Think about sharing what you've heard with your manager (not a co-worker) as a growing concern within the company.
- Encourage those who gossip to go directly to the person who can do something about it instead of simply repeating it to others who have no authority to change it. If you do, you

can create positive solutions for your company rather than being part of the problem in a deteriorating workplace.

Remember, if a gossiper speaks badly of another person, he or she will have a tendency to turn around and speak badly about you.

Don't trust those who gossip. They are destructive forces. Encouraging or supporting them only empowers them to create more drama. Instead of being considered a source of gossip, develop a reputation as someone who can be a trusted confidante.

Want more info? Follow the link about Gossip in the Workplace[14] in the Video Resources section.

# 34
## Are You a Workplace Bully?

Another example of bad workplace conduct is bullying. You might be thinking, "Bullying, in the workplace, really?" Absolutely. Bullying usually involves repeated incidents or a pattern of behavior that is intended to intimidate, offend, degrade or humiliate a particular person or group of people. It has also been described as the assertion of power through aggression. It goes to the mistreatment of those who are not as strong; it also goes to being cruel to others.

### Who Could Be a Bully?

A bully can be the boss who uses intimidation and ridicule to manage his employees; a bully can be someone in a position of power who thinks his or her management style is "authoritarian," and that this is the only way to manage workers, when it's really bullying. A bully can be the manager who unfairly or without reason blocks a worker's promotion, refuses requests for leave, reduces or changes shifts, takes away job responsibilities or blocks opportunities for career or job advancement.

Bullies can be the coworkers who bully to enhance their position or sense of power in the workplace; they use overt physical intimidation or subtle gestures like eye rolling to belittle people, especially in front of others. Bullies can be

111

those who get others in the workplace to side with them against a worker or spread rumors about someone's personal or professional life, either verbally or in texts and emails.

### Who Is at Risk of Being Bullied?
- Young or new workers or apprentices
- Injured workers or those on a return-to-work plan
- Workers (in insecure employment positions) who worry they will lose their job if they complain

### What is the Effect of Bullying in the Workplace?
Bullying doesn't just affect the victim's personal health and well-being. The overall workplace will often experience increased absenteeism, lateness, lost time and staff turnover. Disciplinary or conduct problems will occur. Teamwork will suffer and most likely a decline in respect for management will result because of its allowing bullying to happen. This, in turn, will generate a negative public perception of the organization and its ability to attract workers. Finally, this will lead to inefficient, disrupted or reduced productivity.

### The Keys to Prevent Bullying
If you feel that you are being bullied, discriminated against, victimized or subjected to any form of harassment, there are specific steps that you should take:
- FIRMLY tell the person that his or her behavior is not acceptable and ask him or her to stop. You can ask a supervisor or union member to be with you when you approach the person.
- Keep a factual journal or diary of daily events. Record:

- The date, time and complaint in as much detail as possible.
- The names of witnesses.
- The outcome of the event.

Remember, it's not just the character of the incidents, but the number, frequency and, especially, the pattern that can reveal bullying or harassment.

- Keep copies of any letters, memos, emails, faxes, etc. received from the person.
- REPORT the harassment to the person identified in your employee policy, your supervisor (or his or her manager) or a designated manager. If your concerns are ignored, go to the next management level.
- DO NOT RETALIATE. You may end up looking like the perpetrator and will most certainly cause confusion for those responsible for evaluating and responding to the situation.

Bullying is an unkind act that no one should have to endure. If you experience or witness bullying, take steps to eliminate it from your workplace.

# 35
# Six Things Never to Say at Work

To avoid getting a bad reputation at work, you should avoid stating certain phrases around your boss or coworkers. A little research yielded an article, written by Beth Braccio Hering and featured on CareerBuilder.com, that contained these phrases. I thought that it was so relevant, particularly with the image a person can create, that I wanted to share them with you. These six statements will ruin your reputation, and they come across as whiny, haughty or just downright untrue. My best advice, zip it when it comes to these statements.

**1. "I can't take on any more work. I'm completely overwhelmed already."**

Run your fingers through your hair and let out a big sigh during this lament and colleagues will either nominate you for an Academy Award or provide the number of a good therapist. Professionals work on solving problems, not creating drama.

"Yes, the recession and corporate downsizing has meant fewer people doing more work; however, employers want employees who can manage their workloads and communicate when they have reached their maximum capacity," says Lisa Quast, CEO of Seattle-based Career Woman Inc. and author of *Your Career, Your Way!* "A much better comment is, 'Let's look at my project list and see where

114

we can work this in. It might mean moving something else out to a later date.'"

## 2. "Joe is an idiot."

Yes, maybe he is -- and he may be your boss someday. Don't say something you'll later regret. Even if he doesn't find out, bad-mouthing a co-worker can make listeners wonder what you say about them when they aren't around.

"Never throw your colleagues under the bus or talk about them behind their back," says career coach Roy Cohen, author of *The Wall Street Professional's Survival Guide.* "Colleagues who trust and admire you will be your best support system to promote your reputation as desirable and valuable. When they don't feel that you are transparent in your intentions, your disruptive actions will raise doubts about your ability to be both a team player and a team motivator. Both are essential assets for effective leadership."

## 3. "That's not fair!"

Brad Karsh, president of Chicago-based JB Training Solutions and co-author of the book, *Manager 3.0: A Millennial's Guide to Rewriting the Rules of Management*, notes that this statement is frequently uttered by younger workers. "It may sound harsh, but in the working world, fair does not always mean equal. It can be difficult to understand that at work it's not always fair up and down, but it's also not fair across. For example, a company may hire 100 entry-level employees on the same day. Are they all going to get promoted or receive raises on the same day? No. They may work different hours a week, at different locations and for different types of people. It will never be fair in your career, so get over it."

## 4. "That's not how we did it at my old company."

Make such a comment and colleagues may wonder why you ever left the other employer. As Quast notes, "No one likes an arrogant know-it-all who thinks they're better than others or who believes their previous company did things better." Skip the comparisons and focus instead on articulating your ideas clearly and respectfully.

**5. "I'll have it on your desk by 3 p.m." (when you know you won't)**

Your boss and colleagues have deadlines, too. When you fail to deliver, it affects others. On those rare occasions when you can't fulfill a promise, have the decency to give a heads-up. Deadlines may be changeable or perhaps other workers can shift focus to help out.

"Don't tell people -- whether they are colleagues, vendors, clients and customers or management -- what you think they want to hear instead of the truth," Cohen says. "For example, if you knowingly provide a client with incorrect information about a delivery date and you fail to honor that deadline, you risk tarnishing both your credibility and the reputation of your company. The potential impact may be enormous as customers abandon you for a more reliable provider."

**6. "I'm bored."**

Nothing good ever comes from this statement. Overworked colleague Mary will want to slug you; cubicle neighbor Jeff will think you're a slacker; and your boss will question why he's bothering to give you a paycheck this week.

"There's always something you could be doing," Karsh says. "Take the initiative to tackle new projects; don't wait to be asked to do something. Be innovative and find new projects to work on to make your boss's life easier. Figure out what is keeping your boss up at night, and solve that problem."

## 36
## Office Cubicle Etiquette Has Space for Boundaries

Bad reputations sometimes are earned within the confines of office cubicles. Here's what I mean:

You're sitting in your cubicle at work, busy with a client proposal for the boss. A shrill, irritating cell phone ring pierces the air and interrupts your train of thought. The person in the next cubicle over answers in a loud voice. Suddenly, you hear him jump to his feet and start cursing and screaming. It's the worst! He's rude and inconsiderate beyond belief, and you've spoken to him about it before. You put on your headphones and turn on some music to block the noise and wish for one of those sound-proof cubicles you've heard about. You make a note to ask the boss in your next meeting.

The cubicle world is just the place to show off incredibly poor etiquette! This isn't just a once-and-awhile event but a daily annoyance. Some of the worst behaviors include:

- The loud person whose every word on the phone or to others literally hurts your ears. You can't hear yourself think, must less talk to someone on the phone.

- The chronically ill person who refuses to take a sick day and constantly sneezes and hacks while spreading germs with unwashed hands.
- The "over-sharer" who stops by frequently to tell stories about her personal life that you wish you could wash out of your brain. This can happen several times a day because there are no doors.
- The person in the next cubicle who pops his head up into your space just to see what you're doing.
- The frequent eater who loves food with onions, garlic, fish and pepperoni at his desk.
- Loud personal radios — worse when the person sings along.
- The person who talks to himself out loud all day.
- The chair squeaker.
- The "love bug"who must talk to or have visits from the object of his desire next to you.
- The snoop — the person who goes through the files and drawers of others when they are not around.

**What Should You Do?**

The positive side of cubicles is that they promote teamwork and collaboration by not cutting people off from one another. But, the poor manners of cubicle inhabitants sometimes overcome the positive effects. If you haven't already, suggest to management that they institute some simple rules for employees. For those who can't be handled by management, take some initiative.

- Management should ask everyone to keep their telephone voices at a moderate range. Explain that loud conversations interrupt the work flow of others and lowers productivity of the whole.

- The company should encourage people who are sick to use leave days and don't come to work until they are no longer infectious. When they do return, ask them to use hand sanitizers, wash their hands frequently and don't leave dirty tissue lying around. Management should also encourage employees to work from home when they are well enough to work but still dealing with the residual illness.

- Tell the constant over-sharer that you are too busy to take a break. Turn to your work, hoping he/she will get the hint. If the person doesn't leave, politely explain that you will only be able to visit during breaks. Ignoring the over-sharer will eventually send the right message.

- Management should require that employees take lunch in the lunchroom or out of the office. It's better for employees to take a break, even a short one.

- The company should request employees keep all radios lowered.

- If someone frequently talks or sings to himself/herself and it disturbs you, respectfully tell him/her it bothers you and to please stop. If the person ignores you, speak to your supervisor.

- Offer to use a can of WD-40 on your neighbor's squeaky chair!

- Ask your boss to speak to annoying love birds in the office and ask them not to disturb others with frequent visits. If they continue, tell them they are disturbing you. This goes to a matter of wasting time and productivity, and management should be able to handle it for you.

119

For more information on how to practice good etiquette in your cubicle[15], follow the link in the Video Resources Section.

# 37
# Can Extremely Nice People Be Successful Leaders?

If we're going to avoid all this bad behavior, is there such a thing as being too nice to be successful? In a recent article, authored by Vivian Giang, fellow etiquette coach Barbara Pachter says that nice guys can finish last if they are too polite. From my perspective, my success has been because of my knowledge of etiquette combined with my area of expertise. As a business owner, it is important for employees to enjoy working for you, but there is a fine line between being too nice and not being nice enough!

Pachter says that leaders need to be polite *and* powerful. The danger in being too polite is that employees will eventually stop taking you seriously.

So, what makes the difference between being too polite and being rude? How can you temper it all? Pachter, in her book, *The Essentials of Business Etiquette,* provides 4 simple guidelines to double-check on whether you are being too polite.

**1. Smiling too much.** Constantly having a smile on your face in a business setting makes you appear weaker, less dominant and thus less serious. These may make you easy to work with but won't gain respect. Definitely smile when appropriate, but keep it in check.

**2. Using passive language.** Don't say "I was just wondering" or "Could you perhaps ..." These type phrases make you appear as if you have low self-esteem. Pachter advises that when you begin sentences with "I think" that you are telling others you are unsure about the answer. When giving your opinion, use "I recommend" or "I suggest" which is much stronger.

Review your voice mail messages before sending them to someone. Make sure you convey a message of strength. Don't lead with small talk or use language that makes you appear less in authority.

**3. Apologizing too much.** If you say "I'm sorry" too much, it detracts from your professional image. If you cause a problem, say "I'm sorry" once. Don't keep saying it. That makes you appear unsure of yourself. I prefer to say "I apologize" instead of "I'm sorry."

**4. Not confronting people.** If you're in a leadership position and something is wrong, you need to confront it immediately says Pachter. Some people feel that if they confront others then people won't like them. However, as a leader, it is critical that business issues be addressed in an immediate and straight-forward fashion. People will respect you when you take charge and solve problems. As a leader, never avoid speaking directly to the people involved in a business mistake. If you try to walk around with blinders on, your business will fall apart around you.

This doesn't mean that you should be unfriendly and tough or incredibly demanding. You don't want your employees to be afraid to talk with you, particularly when something is wrong. This will only create problems in the future. You need to create an atmosphere where you are taken seriously while at the same time you are friendly, approachable and people feel they can trust you.

# 38
# How Behavior Affects the Sale – Part 1

## *Before You Meet Clients*

Behavior is paramount in sales. Yet, it is often carelessly overlooked by too many. The next three "chapters" are aimed at reminding all of us the importance of our actions when it comes to sales.

### Phone Facts to Consider
- Who answers the phone?
- How is the phone answered?
- Always answer the phone with a smile on your face.
- Is there a voicemail or answering service?

Oftentimes we're too busy to think about how our phones are answered and the company image that is projected when calls aren't handled professionally. The person answering your phones should be highly trained to do so in a manner that reflects the image you want your company to project. If you use voicemail, make sure that it sounds professional, doesn't have background noise and can be clearly understood.

Did you know that 67 percent of the population do not return or even listen to voice messages? If you're dealing with Millennials, know that they generally ignore voice mail. So, the takeaway is simply to know the generation with which you are dealing and handle accordingly. Does that mean you have to learn to text message if you don't all ready? Probably so. If you are among the 33 percent who return voicemails, or you are placing a call, rehearse what you will say if you get a voicemail. Have notes handy so you aren't caught off guard. There's nothing worse than sounding disjointed or leaving an exceedingly long voicemail. People won't listen to them.

If you use an answering service, provide written instructions on specifically how your calls are to be answered and handled. Don't leave it up to chance. If you do, you may be creating a bad image about your company's abilities.

### When Making Sales Calls

- Return all voice, email and text messages within 24 hours, or have someone do it for you.
- Always place your own calls.
- Speak very professionally.
- Beware of possible background noise.
- Refer to the client by last name until he or she asks to be called by first name, or ask for first-name basis permission after you get to know the person.

### Before Going to a Client Meeting

Think about what you should wear. Here's what you should consider.

- Dress like you care about the client.
- Showing style is good, but be sure your style is understood. A Mother of the Bride requires a different set of clothing than a Wall Street corporate executive.
- Research the dress code of a company before your appointment and dress in that manner. Do this so that those with whom you meet will feel comfortable with you. Once people feel comfortable with you, they can easily accept

you. If they don't feel comfortable, they won't "let you in."

- Make sure your shoes are shined or clean.
- NEVER wear flip flops!
- Do not overdress or underdress.
- Both men and women should keep their jewelry simple. Wearing opulent jewelry may make clients feel like they are paying for it. Being too opulent may make them feel inferior.

Be sure to consider your hygiene. It plays a critical part of the image you create in the mind of a client.

- Make sure your hands are clean. Make sure you have had a manicure and do not have vampire nails.
- Ladies when wearing sandals make sure you have had a pedicure recently. NO CHIPPED NAIL POLISH!
- Always show attention to detail in your appearance.
- Do not wear cologne or perfume. (Did you know that smell is the most powerful connector to memory? Every time I encounter a lady wearing the perfume Taboo, I think of my mother. She always wore that scent, and my memories of her are filled with love. But, what if the person you meet has a negative memory about what you are wearing? Or what if they are allergic?)
- Always wear deodorant. (During stressful moments, it is possible to generate body odor.)
- Make sure your breath is fresh. Always have breath mints on hand.
- Before an appointment, rinse your mouth after eating. Avoid garlic, onions, tuna fish, and heavy spices before meetings.

- If you have an early morning meeting, be careful of the amount of alcohol consumed the night before. (You may reek of it the next day, and that will definitely kill the sale.)
- Make sure your hair is clean and brushed.

**Cars, Social Media and Business Cards**

Consider that what you drive matters. It has the same effect as wearing expensive, flamboyant jewelry. I know sales people who have beautiful, expensive cars but choose to drive mid-priced automobiles when making sales calls or working. I do the same. I have a Lexus, but my MINI Cooper is my working car.

Don't forget about Social Media, particularly Facebook and LinkedIn.

- Be very careful what you post on all social media. (It becomes part of your image. Posting political or religious comments or crude jokes won't win you any points with potential clients. And these days, everyone checks out both potential employees and vendors on social media.)
- Never bad mouth a client or competition on Facebook or in any other way. Once it is on the Internet, it's out there forever and will come back to bite you!
- Keep personal information personal and off social media.

Business Cards

- Keep business cards size to standard. It's frustrating for anyone to deal with oversized cards that won't fit in a card holder or anywhere else. If you are using them to stand out, you'll be standing out in a negative way.
- Adjust font size to your clientele's age. Small fonts are impossible for anyone over 40 to read!

- Present your business card with two hands. It is your identity. Treat it with respect, and your client will too.
- Accept a business card with two hands and READ IT before putting it away. Respect the person's identity.
- If a card has initials that describe a title or certification designation, ask what the initials mean. Use this information for future correspondence or speaking. You will impress the client with your attention to detail.

And finally, before going to any meeting, lay out an agenda for it. Make sure that you have your prospective client's full commitment for the meeting. Ask the client to commit to a specific day and time and ask the client to provide you something specific at that meeting. Explain specifically what your agenda is for the meeting. Want some great advice on how to do that? Read "When Is a Contract Not a Contract?" posted recently at the Extraordinary Events blog. (See Reference Section.) You'll have an entirely new perspective about securing sales meetings with clients.

# 39
# How Behavior Affects the Sale – Part 2

## *Research and Work Appropriate before a Meeting*

We took a look at steps to take before meeting with a prospective client in the last "chapter." Now, let's examine the research and deep thought required in preparation to meet the potential client.

### Know the Client
Knowing the client doesn't just mean having his or her contact information or perhaps even having a past relationship with that person. It is critical that you spend time doing research on that prospect.

- Look up the mission statement of the company.
- Follow the values of the company in conversation and actions. Read press releases on the company site; figure out what the company's priorities are.
- Find the words they use to sell their product and then use those words in both written and spoken correspondence.

- In your first meeting, be prepared to listen far more than you talk.

## Know Your Client's Product

If you are unfamiliar with the company's industry, it is critical that you "bone up" on the vernacular used in the client's industry before the meeting.

- Be sure you say your client's product name(s) correctly. For instance, it's Porsche, not Porsh. Adidas is pronounced Ahh-D-dass, not A-D-diss.
- When you are meeting with a sports team representative, be mindful of the color combinations you wear. Make sure you are not wearing an arch rival's team colors.
- If there is an occasion to send a car to pick up someone from the airport or any destination, make sure the make of the car coincides with the brand they represent. In other words, don't send a Cadillac to pick up a Ford Motor client!

## Preparing Proposals

In a recent article on "Demystifying the Proposal Process and Winning Business without Losing Money," Andrea Michaels, said: "A doctor will not prescribe medication for you without an examination and subsequent diagnosis. A mechanic will not order parts for your vehicle without first examining the car and diagnosing the problem." She goes on to say that while salespeople aren't doctors or mechanics, they often are responsible for fixing a corporate problem. Yet they often rush in without the proper examination and diagnosis.

Michaels asserts that in her own industry of special events, event design and production companies spend $12,000-$15,000 responding to a client's Request for Proposal. To double the pressure, her clients want detail,

detail, detail, including financial statements, and they demand that information immediately.

And, what if you provide all this detail and the client is merely window-shopping? Michaels says, "Why would you want to spend a lot of money with no clue what you are doing?" She affirms, "It would be sheer luck if you could win a bid before you fully understood the needs and goals of your client."

Michaels' solution is firmly aligned with mine. The perfect solution is to charge for your proposal. Like Michaels says, "Most of the companies you are dealing with have R&D departments. They are paid for their time ... This is particularly effective if you know someone is trolling for bids. At the very least, it might keep the competition limited to three instead of 23 bids. Explain to the prospective client that the cost will be refunded upon the signing of a contract (i.e. applied to the sale/job.)"

If your industry requires you to submit bids with advanced details, renderings and complex solutions, Michaels and I agree. "Have clients sign an agreement not to use any part of your proposal if the job is awarded to another company. Do this before you hand over the proposal. Using your ideas is theft. (This will put a stop to the practice of being handed a proposal from a competitor and asked to price it out against them.)"

Both these practices give your proposal far more perceived value.

## 40
## How Behavior Affects the Sale – Part 3

### *During the Meeting*

In Parts 1 and 2 above, we've examined what to do to prepare before meetings with prospective clients. Now, let's take the final step and look at how your behavior will affect the sale during the actual meeting.

One final thought before actually entering the meeting room … Turn off your cell phone <u>before</u> entering any meeting. If you are in a situation of urgency, explain before the meeting starts, set your phone to vibrate and then <u>ONLY</u> accept a call or text pertaining to that situation. <u>IGNORE ALL OTHERS</u>. Accepting calls, text, or emails does not prove how busy you are. It only proves the person on the other end of the device is more important than the person with whom you are sitting. (I've said this before; I'll say it again.) Think about it. How do you feel when you are the person sitting with another and waiting for him or her to end a call or text that has interrupted your meeting?

So, let's imagine you are 5 minutes early to the meeting (as you should be) and have been seated in the client's conference room. If you are male, stand if a lady enters the room. Whether you are male or female, stand when someone senior enters the room. That means someone obviously older than you or of a higher ranking.

**Details you should never overlook in a meeting:**

- Always introduce yourself with a handshake. Ladies make that a firm grip. Make eye contact during the interaction.
- Always introduce the person accompanying you.
- No one works <u>FOR</u> you; they work <u>WITH</u> you. Don't say "John is MY coordinator. "Say "John is The Key Class coordinator." See the difference?
- Body language says 90% more than words can say. Sit up straight, don't slouch and keep your focus directed on the other person. Show interest, listen and pay close attention.
- Do NOT name drop. If the client wants to know with whom you have worked, then let them know.
- Do not try to impress. If you are impressive, it will show. People who have it don't have to prove they have it.
- NEVER discuss personal information about past clients with ANYONE. It does not impress people. It makes them worry what you will say about them.
- NEVER make disparaging remarks about others. Knocking someone down does not bring you up. Compliment the competition at all costs, and then throw up later.
- Remember the magic words! PLEASE AND THANK YOU.
- When visiting a client's office, (before sitting down with them) take in the décor. Comment

on photographs and awards or special art. People appreciate your noticing the details. Shows how observant and detail-oriented you are.

- If you are given another person's proposal to follow, <u>refuse</u>. Would you want someone to do that to you?

**The Key Golden Rule to never forget:**

Rudeness is a Weak Man's Imitation of Strength How you treat all others – employees, a waitperson in a restaurant, fellow team members and peers – reflects who and what you are. Never talk down to anyone. Never assume it doesn't go unnoticed.

**When dining or entertaining prospects or clients:**

- Always be careful with the amount of alcohol you consume. One cocktail before dinner and one glass of wine with dinner PERIOD.
- Over-drinking makes you vulnerable. Remain in control of your faculties.
- Order good quality wine but not excessive in cost.
- You don't want the client feeling that he or she will be paying for it in the end.

**In the end, remember to:**

- Always tell the client that you want their business and will do anything it takes to satisfy them.
- Say this no matter how long the relationship has lasted between you and the client.
- If you make a mistake, own it! You will gain far more respect than trying to shove a mistake under the rug or blaming someone else.

- Going after business is not showing off how successful you are. It is how successful you can make your client. So, **be humble!** You are there to serve.

So much of sales is developing personal relationships. If you adopt and maintain the behavior outlined in this short series, you will find clients willing and eager to work with you and make many friends along the way!

# 41
## Taming the Angry Caller

Another tool to have in your Workplace Conduct Kit is how to tame an inflamed customer. Read on to learn more.

The phone rings; you pick it up, and the voice on the other end begins screaming at you. What should you do? My first thought is to bite my tongue, stay calm and listen. Let the person vent and blow off steam. Don't interrupt ... even with a solution before he or she tells his or her story. Don't raise your voice. Take it down a notch. Speak softly to show that you're interested in handling the caller's complaint in a calm, rational way.

If the caller is a client and ranting about poor service or an unsatisfactory product, be patient, listen, use phrases like "I understand how you feel." It's important to empathize, never interrupt and always apologize. Why? Because that's what the caller wants to hear ... that you are sorry for offering a poor service or product. However, avoid the words "I'm sorry." Instead, use "I apologize." Why? Because the latter has an air of finality about it.

Let the caller know how you plan to make amends. For example: "I apologize for the inconvenience caused. I will have one of our reps call you in the next 30 minutes. If you'd like to leave your number with me, I'll call later in the day to check on the progress." Always be professional, but let the caller know you're not a pushover.

It's all right to ask the caller to take his or her tone down a notch. Toning it down and speaking softly are the best defenses for tempering a bad mood. Also, slowing down the caller helps him or her think more clearly about his or her choice of words. I'll say, "Would you please repeat that a little slower, because you're running your words together and I'm not sure what exactly you're trying to say.'"

Avoid doing anything to inflame an angry caller further. Most of the time, angry callers have legitimate complaints and have reached the end of their rope. Take the tack of being very empathetic with angry callers. They can sense quickly whether you are a consumer advocate or not.

If someone gets personal or abusive, caution him or her to stick to the topic and try to let you help.

Find value in what the person has told you. No matter what, there is value; this tells your caller that you see value in them and in their message. This, along with following other good listening skills, builds trust and respect, and reduces the fear that may be the basis for the outburst.

This is always a great opportunity to fix the problem beyond the client or customer's expectations. When we go above and beyond what is expected, something interesting happens. The customer will often become a more loyal customer, and that loyal customer will share his or her experience with others.

So often it's tempting to place blame on a colleague when dealing with an angry call. The customer does not care who made the mistake. They just want it fixed.

**Using 4 Key Ps when Dealing with a Difficult Customer or Question**

- Pause — Give customers a chance to get all their words out before you say anything.

- Paraphrase — Make sure you know exactly what the problem is.
- Probe — Ask more questions. Dig deeper.
- Provide response — Sometimes you may not want to provide the response right away, especially if you know the customer won't like the response.

The overall key is to respect the caller, listen and resolve the issue. Never escalate. The results won't be pretty if you do.

Use the link in the Video Resources section for "6 Ways to Get an Angry Customer to Back Down."[16]

# 42
# Gift Exchange Ideas for the Holidays

I pondered whether to include this information. However, I get so many questions from people about what to do about gift ideas in the office around holiday time that I think it will be useful, particularly because these aren't just every-day ideas. And, it all goes back to making others feel good about you.

Most everyone is familiar with Secret Santa and White Elephant gift exchanges at office and holiday parties. For the season, I wanted to search around and find some unique or fun ideas to offer up and get everyone's creative juices flowing. It's not always easy to come up with new ideas, so here are some I gleaned from *Business News Daily* to share with you.

### Charity Exchange

Of course I would think of this first, and so did my resource. In lieu of presents, get everyone in the office to share their favorite charity, along with their names, and put it in a hat. Have everyone select a name. The outcome? Each employee gives a small donation with a money limit to the charity drawn.

## Gift Auction

This can instigate some fun competition. Each employee brings a gift that is put on display in the office. Each employee is assigned a number of points (like 100 or 200) to bid on gifts as each is presented.

The auction should go as long as it takes for each employee to use up the allotted points given and everyone has won a gift.

This can be done as a live or silent auction. With a silent auction, have employees bid points on clipboard forms placed in front of each gift. The final bid (bidding is timed) wins.

Silent auctions can also be done with small ballots in boxes in front of each gift so no one has the advantage of seeing what others have bid.

## Gift Grab

Have everyone bring a small, wrapped gift within a certain price range and place it in a specified area. Assign a number to each person participating and put the numbers in a hat. Ask each person to draw a number to determine the order in which they may select a gift.

However, a gift grab allows people to steal gifts after they have been chosen by others. For instance, once the first person has gone, anyone after that can choose to either take another person's present or choose from the pile. The person whose gift is stolen can do the same — either steal another's gift or pick a new one — but they cannot steal back their gift.

Play until there are no gifts left to exchange.

## Coffee Mugs

Because almost everyone has a use for a coffee mug, limit your employees to exchanging funny or decorative coffee mugs. Everyone can draw names from a hat. Set a price limit. To make it even more fun, suggest employees fill their mugs with treats (like candy, teas or hot cocoa packets.)

### Book Exchange

Have an office filled with people who love to read? Have each employee bring in a copy of his or her favorite book, or a book by his or her favorite author. Draw names from a hat to decide who gets which book.

To make this even more meaningful, have employees write a note to the recipient explaining why the particular gift book is so special to them. This is inexpensive but allows employees to learn more about one another and perhaps discover similar interests.

### Recipe Baskets

Almost everyone has a favorite recipe. Exchange your favorite recipes instead of actual presents. Suggest employees make a gift basket with instructions and the ingredients to make the dish. Again, to determine who should get each basket, simply draw names out of a hat and let individuals take the basket belonging to the name that has been drawn.

### Co-worker Trivia

This is a great way to help your employees learn even more about each other. Have everyone bring a wrapped gift under a certain price limit and put them in an area where you will all gather later.

Ask each employee to write down a little-known fact about himself or herself on an index card. Have the president of the company draw the cards one at a time and read the fact aloud. The first person who guesses the name of the employee to which the fact belongs gets to select a present.

Keep this going until all presents have been collected. And, everyone will know each other better as well.

Hopefully, you can take these ideas to your office manager as suggestions to liven up a gift exchange. In addition, keep the following in mind:

- Involve the entire office. This should apply to the entire staff.
- Cap the cost per gift. Decide beforehand on the maximum dollar amount ($10-$15) to be spent on gifts, which will spare your employees budgets during this expensive time of year.
- Give advance notice. If you're involving your office in an organized gift exchange, inform people well in advance so everyone has time to shop.
- Schedule accordingly and before people leave early for holidays. Rather than during a holiday celebration when clients might attend, consider a small pre-holiday reception in the office.
- Urge common sense. Suggest gifts not be inappropriate, sexually suggestive or otherwise problematic. Instruct employees to take extra care.

# 43
# How to Avoid Being Thrown Under the Bus

Have you ever or are you currently experiencing getting thrown under the bus at work? Maybe another person uses his or her position of power over you more than necessary? This behavior creates animosity, doesn't it? What about a manger who never takes responsibility for mistakes and, instead, blames them all on you? Let's say that these mistakes are rarely yours, but are the result of the manager's inability to utilize the information which you have provided him or her.

**What are the best responses to being thrown under the bus?**

Let's start with that "thing" I keep harping about: Attitude.

**Maintain a positive attitude.**

Seriously, your attitude will make or break any situation. Instead of complaining and making everyone else around you miserable, maintain a positive attitude. Jack Canfield's *Key to Living the Law of Attraction: A simple guide in Creating the Life of Your Dreams* asserts this as well. So remember you can't change other people's behavior or attitude, but you can certainly take control of the way you handle situations.

**Write yourself a letter or take it out of the office to vent.**

It's difficult to just take bad behavior from others. It's not healthy to internalize that type of angst, which can cause stress, physical or mental health problems. You need to vent at some point, so do so by writing a letter in response to the unfair treatment you are receiving. Throw it all out there in the letter, and then don't send it. Just delete it. Abraham Lincoln did this often. And, if you'll recall, he's remembered as a great President and human being.

Another method is to take it outside of the office and talk to a friend, family member or designated counselor. Never vent to a co-worker. Express you anger, talk it out, but keep it out of the workplace. If you do go with this approach, the person serving as your counselor may have effective ideas to help you deal with the issues.

**Conduct yourself with professionalism.**

Because you are not responsible for the actions of others doesn't mean you aren't responsible for your own behavior. The way you behave will affect your current and future career opportunities. People who blame others for their own mistakes tend to believe that it is "every man for himself." Don't let this person "get to you." Instead, maintain grace under pressure. Take the high road and maintain your professionalism. Quietly document all your procedures and work load to have proof of what you have done in each instance. Trust that those around you, and those higher up in the organization, will clearly compare your behavior to that of the person constantly throwing you under the bus.

**Look at the situation as an opportunity to learn.**

Look at this situation as a learning opportunity to grow and develop knowledge you wouldn't have otherwise experienced. It will be a challenge but one you can handle if you adjust your attitude and maintain your cool. If you respond negatively and explode in anger, the person who threw you under the bus ultimately wins. Don't let him. Instead, determine what you have learned and how you can put that lesson to good use in the future. The goal here is not to focus on the situation but rather how you handled the situation.

**Additional Great Tips**

Greg Baker, President and CEO of Advance Consulting, offers some great advice on how to avoid being thrown under the bus:

- **Anticipate Conflict**: In my coaching work with executives I spend a lot of time helping them anticipate conflict and attacks as they navigate the political waters. It is unfortunate that executives have to spend so much time thinking about this, but that's another article. While the typical executive has a big need here, this applies to everyone at every level in the organization. Here are some suggestions:
  - **Recognize Circumstances That Breed Conflict**: I have never seen someone get thrown under the bus when everything was going well. So as you develop your radar for potential conflict, let this be your guidepost. When things go wrong, some people tend to blame in order to protect themselves.
  - **Identify Blamers**: Identify people who are inclined to blame and keep your eye on them when you find yourself in the same "sandbox" as them when things go wrong.

- o **Anticipate Risky Situations**: Anticipate when circumstances are heading toward trouble and, if possible, avoid them.
- o **Understand Other People's Inclinations**: Go to school on people and understand what they are capable of and willing to do. For example, if you see someone throwing a person under the bus, they are most likely capable and willing to do the same thing to you.
- o **Be Prepared to Deal With Conflict**: Just as someone who practices martial arts prepares to handle conflict if it arises, you can do things to prepare for conflict in a work environment.

- **Do Your Job**: First and foremost, keep your own house in order. Know your responsibilities, do your job, and keep evidence of your accomplishments in case you need it.
  - o **Build Relationships**: One way you can partially guard against getting thrown under the bus is to build relationships with people before any bus throwing begins. People are less likely to betray a friend, but don't take that as a guarantee.
  - o **Resolve Problems Early**: If you involve others to solve a common problem, you can often avoid conflict before it happens. Go after and resolve the core issue together and build teamwork instead of letting conflict just happen.
  - o **Be Ready to Advocate for Yourself**: If you find yourself under the bus, you may have to advocate for yourself. Make your case, compile your evidence, and present it clearly to those involved and those up the chain who need to know.

According to Baker, none of us can avoid the bus 100% of the time. He suggests that if you practice anticipating and preparing to deal with conflict, you can avoid a lot of it. He goes on to say you shouldn't overdo it either because if you find yourself spending too much time in a defensive posture your productivity may be suffering. Finally, Baker suggests you re-evaluate and find the right balance, and above all else, practice peaceful resolution – we need more of that in the world.

## 44
## How to Quit Your Job

Want to quit your job? Feel like marching into your boss' office and yelling "I quit," and then picking up your possessions and walking right out the door?

Of course, you wouldn't do that. Logic tells you that is a rude way to handle resigning.

So, what is the right way to behave when you want to leave your job?

### Talk to Your Manager First

Don't talk about your decision to resign to anyone else before you talk to the boss. Imagine how difficult it would make this transition if your manager heard this from someone else other than you. Be willing to work with him or her about the timing of your leaving, dependent upon the needs of the company.

Discuss how your departure will be communicated to the rest of the company at that time. There are a variety of scenarios. It can be announced at a meeting; you could be responsible for informing the key people in your organization. What about announcing it in an email?

It's best not to let rumors, which can be exaggerated, start through the organization. So work out those details with your boss.

147

### Two Weeks' Notice

Two weeks is generally the norm. Anything else is inconsiderate.

But be willing to work with the organization and its needs unless you have a commitment to another company to which you need to adhere. Remember that the more responsibility you have and the higher you are in the organization will make it more difficult to replace you. In that case, you may need to train your replacement, so before making a commitment to another company, consider that a month's notice might be more appropriate.

However, much more than that might be unwise. Once you've resigned, everyone else will consider you a "short-timer" and will potentially exclude you from team meetings, which will make it more difficult for you to function effectively.

### Be Honest

Once you've resigned, it won't be long before your other team members know where you've landed. You will want to maintain the relationships you've built.

Networking and relationships are the key to success in business. So, while you don't have to tell everyone where you are going and what you will be doing, if you do, it will be easier to keep those relationships.

Be straight with everyone. Don't create different "versions" of your reasons for leaving, i.e. "I hate this place and can't wait to leave" as opposed to "I got an offer from another company that I couldn't resist." This will only create gossip and leave a bad impression.

### Leave a Positive, Lasting Impression

No matter why you've decided to leave the company, it is important not to neglect how your leaving will affect your company. Your final responsibility is to work with your boss for direction and management of how you should bring your work load to a close.

Don't leave any loose ends. You want your former employer, managers and coworkers to have a positive impression of you. That means being an ultimate professional to the end.

### Be Grateful

Remember that even if you are thrilled to be leaving, you had experiences from which you learned and which will add to your area of expertise. So, be grateful. Be appreciative. Consider writing notes of gratitude to your boss and team members. Even if your manager or those who reported directly to you act as if you have betrayed them, soldier through it. Try to change their minds. Be gracious. This will add to the positive image you leave with them.

### Exit Interview

You might want to unload and give your opinion of everything that is wrong with the company. You know, things you wished you would have said when you were an employee.

But there's danger there. You are never guaranteed anonymity, and unfortunately, it won't change the nature of the organization.

Try to be positive about the people in the organization. If you had good experiences, say so. If you have constructive criticism (no venting), then offer it in a professional and encouraging manner.

### Leave the Past Behind

After leaving your former job, never badmouth the company or any of its employees.

If people ask why you left your previous job, just tell them it was not a great fit. Making disparaging remarks about a former employer or co-workers in a job interview will only convince future employers that you will do the same to them.

149

Whatever your grievances, even if they are deserved, don't go there with others in the future. Remain professional, and that is how others will see you. Anything else won't win you any influence.

### Keys to Remember

- Give at least two weeks' notice and offer to work longer to create a smooth and orderly transition if your schedule allows.
- Work with your boss to figure out the best use of your remaining days and how to close out your responsibilities.
- Be grateful for what you learned at your job and openly express gratitude to colleagues.
- Don't give different reasons to different people — stick to one story about why you're leaving.
- Don't be dishonest about your next move — everyone will find out soon enough.
- Don't vent or be emotional in the exit interview. Stay positive.
- Don't bad mouth your former company or any of its employees.
- Use the link in the Video Resources section to see How to Quit your Job with Class.[17]

# IMAGE BUILDING

# The Importance of Image Building

I recall when I opened my first business in 1976 that I was broke but had an idea I was sure could work. I wanted to open a business that would do events only. Yes, we would do décor, catering and entertainment but focus on events only.

I borrowed $500.00 from a dear friend that had a great deal of faith in me. I took $250.00 of that loan and went out and purchased two very expensive outfits. I treated those two outfits like they were gold, because they were. They were my first key to success.

I drove an old, battered Ford van. It still worked fine and was all that I could afford. To not embarrass myself in front of clients, I would get ready to go visit my top-of-the-line wealthy prospects in one of my outfits and drive my old van near to the meeting site. Then, I would park two blocks away and walk to the actual meeting location.

I did not want anyone seeing what I was driving, but I did want them to see that I could afford expensive clothing which in my mind made me look successful. Because I felt like I looked successful, I acted the part and had an air of confidence about me. Don't confuse that look with arrogance. I walked into an appointment, and it worked. Wealthy people can smell money and see when you are wearing it. My outfits and attitude gave them enough confidence in me to give me their business.

Soon I had photographs of events I'd produced for the best names in Los Angeles to add to my "package."

This was my first experience with building a positive identity. I later got a wonderful piece of advice from the same friend who had given me the loan (which I paid back quickly after winning contracts) when I became more successful. The advice? Be careful of the car you drive when you meet with clients. Clients don't want to see you drive up to their homes in an expensive car, because the first thing they will think is "Am I paying for that car?" Buy a Bentley, but keep it in the garage for the weekends and not for days that you are working. Keep you image classic rather than ostentatious.

Depending on where you are going you will want to be flexible with your image and make sure that you are wearing something that will make you fit in, not stand out. For example, I had a meeting with corporate executives at Gap headquarters. I was dressed to the "nines" with suit, tie, nice shoes and belt. Upon entering, I noticed corporate team members were dressed in business casual attire. Then it hit me! I was overdressed and off-brand! I immediately ran to the restroom, took off my coat and tie, opened my shirt collar and ruffled my hair a bit. I then threw my jacket over my shoulder, added a bit of swagger to my walk when I entered the marketing department, and went in to meet the execs. I fit right in. The last thing I wanted to do was not understand their branding and not fit into their environment. I was twice the age of almost everyone working at Gap, so I needed to display that "I may be old but I do have style and can help." By the way, I got Gap as a client, and we worked together for many years.

People are most confident speaking with those with whom they can relate. The first way they will know is by the way you look. Some people may take issue with this because they don't feel they are being themselves if they dress a certain way. I have even had people comment that they feel it is dishonest. However, I think it is plain smart.

153

The next Section in this "book of hints" is meant to share further ideas on the true meaning of a positive identity when it comes to YOU. I hope you will enjoy it and make notes with what you may want to do for your identity.

## 45
## Image Builders vs. Image Killers

**Image Builders Up Close and Personal**

Not long ago, I polled fellow etiquette coaches to determine what they felt, beyond appearance, was the No. 1 most important image-building characteristic. Trustworthiness, confidence, empathy, charisma, compassion and genuineness were all mentioned. But by majority, here were the Top 5 image builders.

- Your smile — Your willingness and readiness to smile. It is the single most evident indication of your brand. It reveals you are friendly, warm and inclusive. And, it is the universal language that prompts a smile back. It disarms, solves problems, reverses negative situations and is healing.

- Body language (goes with the smile, doesn't it?) — Having a positive attitude supports and encourages others without judgment. This includes posture, which shows you are confident whether walking into a meeting or social situation. When seated, erect posture can reveal your participation by listening and trying

155

to understand. Leaning into the conversation and then slightly back shows engagement. Listening, drawing back and thinking, then leaning forward again, always erect, feet flat on the floor, shoulders back. Remember, if you can't walk across a room with a book balanced on your head, you need to improve your posture. Body language, in addition to a smile, includes eye contact. And, think about where your arms are. If they are crossed, are they acting as a barrier to the other person?

- We kept going back to Maya Angelou's quote: "People will forget what you said, people will forget what you did, but people will never forget how you made them feel." Being able to make someone feel good about themselves when they are with you is a wonderful talent that will leave people with an incredible image of you.

- Combined with how you make others feel, the ability to listen carefully and respond to the other person's needs makes you the smartest person in the room.

- Self-esteem and confidence were at the top of our list. Combine that with the ability to honor one's own uniqueness to shape energy into success. If your goal is to be received as part of a team, then create an image that "fits" with the majority of the team, and participate in ways that can be received. Smiling and helping other to feel good are useful here. If your goal is to lead a group of people to success, then support yourself in being an inspiring person who helps people feel received and honored for the resources they contribute — set expectations and stretch objectives and stay true to your own willingness to succeed. Let your self-esteem and confidence be role models for others.

**Image Killers Online**

If we employ the characteristics above to build image, it is critical that we don't undermine that image on social media. The group discussed the best ways to kill your image using social media. Here are the Top 4 killers.

- The use of hate speech, sexist or racial slurs followed by overly polarizing political/religious commentary. These can create an image crisis from which one may not ever truly recover.

- The use of profanity. Someone who presents in real life and in professional settings as appropriate, well-spoken and pulled-together can truly undermine his/her credibility by cutting completely loose on social media.

- Inappropriate or embarrassing photos with comment threads that get out of hand.

- Giving out too much information, including trivia, which is of no interest to others, such as what you are doing or thinking at the moment. Example: "I think I will eat a cupcake;" "I am at the dentist;" "My stomach hurts."

The Key to building both your personal and professional image is consistency across all "platforms." Think of image-building like you would branding a product.

Understand that the most successful brands stay within the boundaries of what you have come to admire about them, and let that be your guide.

## 46
## Simple Tips to Help You Master the Art of Body Language for Business and Life

Part of image-building is being able to connect to others. Connecting to a person means making it clear how the content of a spoken message should be interpreted. Unfortunately, sometimes we are unable to deliver our messages by spoken or even written language, so we use body language to supplement what we want to say by gesturing, moving or making facial expressions.

Our body language sends a message to the other person, saying things like, "I'm bored and uninterested," or "I'm interested and excited to be here." No matter what words you use, your body language will always give you away. The body doesn't lie!

To be a successful body language communicator, keep the following in mind:

### Sitting
Take care in the way you sit, for no other position connotes so much on its own. Think of the diversity of sitting positions that you've seen in business meetings, from practically horizontal to alert and upright. Sit upright. Never slouch. Sit with a straight back and with your legs together in

front of you or crossed, either at the knee or at the ankle. Normally, women don't cross their legs, but men are allowed to. Avoid jiggling your knee, which is a sign of nervousness (and can be pretty annoying to people sitting near you). Keep your hands away from your face. Always face the person with whom you are speaking or to whom you are listening. If you don't, you'll come across as uninterested. Think of it as trying to impress someone you're interested in. Think about making yourself bigger and puffing out your chest.

### Standing

When you stand, keep your back straight, with your midsection in alignment with your back (shoulders back and head up). This shows that you are comfortable with yourself and at ease in the situation. Slouching, sticking your belly out, stuffing your hands in your pockets and folding your arms defensively all suggest aggressive unease. When you slouch with your arms folded across your chest, you give the impression that you are tired, defensive and uninterested.

### Hands

Some people talk with their hands; others stand with their hands glued to their sides. Most people haven't the foggiest notion what their hands are doing when they talk. Do you scratch your nose, your ears or your eyelids when speaking? All of these can be a sign of deception. Other movements to avoid include pointing fingers, wringing your hands, knuckle cracking, picking your fingernails and playing with your pocket change. If you talk with your hands, you're going to come across as distracted or nervous. Keep your hands at your sides, or place them in your lap if you don't know what to do with them.

Rubbing the chin or placing the hand under the chin with one or two fingers on the cheek is a sign of contemplation or evaluation.

Using your hands is effective sometimes, aggressive other times and irrelevant most of the time. Controlling your hands takes effort and willpower. Monitor your hand movements. Avoid making sweeping, cappuccino-clearing gestures during meetings. If you have to, sit on your hands!

**Head Movements**
Head movements communicate important information. Nodding in agreement can be immensely helpful to others, but too much nodding makes you look like a bobble-head doll! Shaking your head can signal disagreement or disapproval. Avoid shaking your head too much.

**Eye Contact**
Eye contact is critical to conveying that you are interested. Letting your gaze wander around the room illustrates disinterest. Looking at your lap or the floor shows that you are not self-confident and feel insecure. Looking someone directly in the eyes while speaking with him or her will assure the other person of your self-esteem, confidence and ability to get the job done. It also conveys trust.

**Smile**
Nothing can make a person feel better than a smile from another. To brighten someone's day and show off your positive attitude, smile. A frown will always set the wrong tone. (Is there a repeating theme here?)

**3 Keys or Tells to Help You in Business**
- To spot a lie, look for hand or face touching, crossed arms and leaning away.
- To reach an agreement, smile, nod, or mirror the other person.
- To maximize your authority, minimize movements. Take a deep breath, bring your

gestures down to waist level, and pause before making a key point.

To watch a great video on body language, follow the link[18] to Amy Cuddy's TED talk in the Video Resources Section.

# 47
## Go Hand-to-Hand with Success

You can't see it right now, but my arm is outstretched to shake your hand. Close your eyes and go with it.

Before I shake your hand, let me tell you how the handshake originated. Around 2500 B.C. in Egypt, men began to extend their right hands to indicate that they meant no harm and held no weapon. It makes sense when you think about it. Truly a friendship gesture.

So, what's all the hub-bub about shaking hands properly? Have you ever shaken someone's hand and felt like you were hanging on to a limp fish? What about the time your fingers were crushed by an over-zealous and very large man? Then, there's the guy who pumps your hand and arm so hard that you think you could have kick-started 20 lawn mowers! Knowing how to properly shake another person's hand will make a great first impression. It's imperative in business and just the right thing to do socially. Remember good manners boils down to two things: respect for others and making them feel comfortable when they're around you. And it's part of creating your image from the get-go.

So, here's how. Always stand to meet or greet someone who is standing. Put your lead foot forward. Extend the right hand and grasp the other person's hand firmly. Remember, no wimpy, fish handshakes. Grasp firmly but don't be too harsh.

Make sure the skin between forefinger and thumb meets the other person's. If you're seated in a crowed area, then there is an exception, so smile and make eye contact instead.

### Meet and Greet

Then, introduce yourself. Look the person you're greeting directly in the eyes. "Hello, Mr. Garcia, I'm John Daly." Hopefully, the person I'm greeting will reply, "It's a pleasure to meet you, Mr. Daly. I'm Joe Garcia."

(This is my chance to get on a first-name basis.) I say, "Please call me John, Mr. Garcia." (That's his cue to say it is all right to use his first name. If he doesn't say so, continue to call him Mr. Garcia.)

Follow the link[19] in the Video Resources Section for a visual look at properly shaking hands.[19]

### 5 Keys to a Successful Handshake
- Simplified, use these five keys:
- Firm grip
- Eye contact until you let go of each other's hands
- Lead foot forward so you are in balance
- Web of the hand from index finger to thumb connect
- Stand if sitting when introduced

Practice it with family members. Do so until each of you is comfortable with the way it feels.

# 48
# The Likeability Factor, and How You Can Improve Yours

Part of having a great image is being likeable. So, I read with interest an article by Bruce Kasanoff, who writes for entrepreneurs. He says that the most attractive quality a person can possess is to be utterly comfortable with who they are. So, if you want people to like you, be 100 percent comfortable in your own skin. He says this quality transcends physical appearance, intelligence, education, income or personality and that it is the cornerstone of success in business and in life.

Because (Kasanoff says) that a person's internal comfort level is not fixed, you can change it. To do that, he says, you must do three things.

**1.** Accept the qualities you cannot change. Kasanoff warns not to waste energy on things such as how your parents raised you or whether you are too short.

**2.** Recognizing your ability to change is *far* greater than you once thought. You can't change your height, but you can change how hard you work, how grateful you are for your blessings, how open you are to new ideas, how you approach difficult challenges, and how willing you are to pay the price for what you most want in life.

**3.** Be persistent. Kasanoff warns that it takes time to build confidence and competence, and suggests investing the time, even on days when you feel as though you are sliding backward.

But in addition to not being insecure, I want to take this further. You can build your likability by:

- Being considerate of others. When you think about the comfort of others first, you're going to appear very likable in their eyes.
- Being grateful for what you have. Being grateful translates to happiness, and a happy person is more prone to be likable than a complainer.
- Maintaining a positive attitude. Positive people boost the mood of others around them. In return, people love to hang around people with positive energy. Negativity abounds in our world — in the news, in social media and from others. Being positive will make you a pleasure to talk to and more people will want to talk to you.
- Staying genuine. Likable people never try to be something they aren't. They admit when they don't know something or if they make a mistake. If they don't agree with someone else's statement, they are quick to admit that they don't see the issue in the same way, and they do so without making the other person feel badly about himself or herself.
- Not judging. When you are judgmental, people can sense it. Even if you smile and hide your negative feelings, the people around you can sense that you have just formed a poor opinion of them. Rather than seeing others as good or bad, try to understand that everyone is entitled to their own opinions, choices, and mistakes. Likable people make this their philosophy and, as long as no one is getting hurt, they never pass

judgment on the value or morality of another person.

- Not competing. Likable people never one-up in a conversation. Instead, they view conversations as an opportunity to connect and create deep relationships with others. If you want to be more likable, enter every conversation with the goal to make the other person feel liked and respected. This will change the tone of the interactions you have, and make everyone involved more likely to enjoy it.
- Providing value. When someone complains about a situation, don't go along with it and talk about some awful situation of your own. Recognize that the other person has a problem that needs solving. People everywhere have problems they wouldn't mind help solving. But as people, we tend to be self-involved and not notice. If you take notice and help people solve their problems, you'll create friends for life.
- Touching others. Don't be afraid to pat someone on the shoulder, shake hands or, depending upon the situation, hug others. It will make others more comfortable around you. Touching eliminates the physical barrier of distance and eliminates the emotional barrier that the distance represents. It may seem awkward at first, but practice it. Others will respond in a positive manner.
- Developing deep conversations. Small talk doesn't develop long-lasting friendships or make you more likable. Show a genuine interest in others, ask honest questions to help further your understanding of them and relate to what they've told you. Don't settle for small

talk. Move the conversation forward to more personal subjects.

Think back to the last time you interacted with a really likable person. What did that person say or do that made you warm to him or her? Remember, at some point, most likable people decided to work at becoming more engaged, more respectful and more likable. Now they seem to work magic and develop friendships wherever they go.

You can seem like that, too! Just develop the habits above.

# 49
# How to Create Your Personal Image

Creating an image in the business world for a business or individual isn't as difficult as you think! But it requires a concentrated effort.

When a brand is built for a company, it happens from the ground up. It is about appearance as well as what is being said. It's critical to put out to the public what people want to hear. Just as important is keeping things (like profanity, rudeness, harsh criticism of others) that you do not want them to hear under close guard.

So how can building business brand concepts apply to building an individual image?

## Appearance
Businesses use billboards for their products, and people use clothing, hair styles and personal hygiene. It's important to convey just the right message. If you think of your body as a billboard, consider how you present it. Remember when you get a tattoo that it lasts for a lifetime unless you go through a painful laser procedure to take it off. If you must have a tattoo, put it where you can hide it.

### How Do You Make Others Feel?

When you create your image, remember that a brand is a feeling.

- How do you feel when you see advertisements for the Hawaiian Islands? Relaxed?
- How do you feel when you see an ad for Ralph Lauren clothing. Luxury?
- How do you feel when you see happy couples on an online dating service commercial? Lonely, yet hopeful?

How do people feel when they see you? You hold the key to that. It is up to you to make your brand. You make that brand when you walk out of your front door. Do you want flash and dash or a conservative feeling to come from a person seeing you at 10 feet away?

What about the message you present? Always make believe a person cannot hear what you have to say before you meet them and prepare your "package" for that. You may be the most talented person in the world in any given field but *first* you have to sell yourself. Save the talent for the big surprise.

Are you polite? Do you give up your chair for an older person? Do you open the door for a person you are hosting? Do you smile? So many people don't smile; they frown instead! This is very off-putting. Develop a ready, genuine smile that will help you connect positively with others in any situation. (Again, a recurring theme!)

Don't let social anxieties overwhelm you. Smiling can help you get through any situation. It's a secret weapon that totally disarms people and draws them to you.

### What Messages Are You Emitting?

In addition to watching what you post on social media, what about the way you act? Create positive trends and habits that draw positive people to you. You can accomplish this through your stylish dress; encouraging and outgoing actions;

and willingness to help others. Self-absorption will only produce a negative reaction in most people. Don't know how to be outgoing with others? Start by volunteering some time to help those less fortunate than you. You'll quickly learn that your life is fairly wonderful compared to others, and this will teach you how to reach out and encourage other people.

**Create Your Image Early**

Marketing yourself later in life will be a lot easier if you have already made a statement at school or college with not only your family and friends but your community. Honoring and respecting others is the greatest tool you can have in your self-image toolbox. Part of honoring and respecting others is taking responsibility for not only your actions but also for part of your own livelihood.

These aren't the only suggestions you should utilize to create a solid image for yourself, but they are the foundation for creating and managing everything else you do as you build a professional business image for yourself and create and perpetuate your company's brand.

Use the link in the Video Resources Section to view "How to Create a Hot Personal Brand."[20]

# 50
# Your Cell Phone and the Impression You Make with It

This may be a little repetitive, but it is such a problem in our society that it is worth repeating when it comes to your image. I've mentioned various portions of the following information throughout this book, but I wanted you to have it all in one place.

So, what does your voicemail message say about your image? If I call you and get, "This is James; catch you later," what kind of impression have you given me? Your message should reflect a professional tone with a concise message. Do you want a potential client or boss to be greeted with "Catch you later"?

I suggest something like, "Hi, this is James. I'm sorry I can't take your call right now, but if you leave me your name and telephone number I will get back to you as soon as possible. Thanks for calling."

In addition, I propose checking your ringtones to be sure they are standard. When in the company of a prospective employer or clients, always set phones on silent or vibrate.

It's important to realize that the people you are with should always take precedent over phone calls or text messages. Some key phone etiquette to remember:

- Let your voicemail take your calls while meeting with people (business or friends).
- Return all phone calls within 24 hours.
- Do not make or receive calls during business meetings.
- If you are expecting an important call that cannot be postponed, alert the people in your meeting prior to the start of the situation; if and when you receive the call, step away from the meeting and keep the call brief.
- Always be courteous to people within hearing distance and use discretion when discussing private matters. Keep your voice low.
- When receiving a call in a restaurant, always step outside or to a place of privacy.
- Do not use your cell phone for talking or texting while driving unless you have a Bluetooth device.
- Never text while in motion.
- Text messaging while in a meeting should only be used in extreme circumstances and emergencies.
- Never text message during religious services, funerals, weddings, court proceedings or while sitting at a dining table.
- If you receive a text message about an urgent matter, remove yourself from your surroundings before answering.

When I go to meetings, my cell phone stays in the car. If I think I might need it to provide contact information during the meeting, it stays in my pocket on vibrate or turned off. I don't let anything disturb me unless it's critical. Then I keep it on vibrate and ask others to forgive me: "I might receive a critical call related to a current project and have to be available. Please understand."

I certainly understand when others are in that position. But when they're not, I'm so put off when people with whom I'm at a meeting start taking calls or messages during my time with them. Taking phone calls or texting others tells those you are with that they aren't as important to you as the person on the phone.

Sometimes we aren't aware of the negative impressions we create for others. When you are trying to spend quality time with friends and associates or trying to be attentive during a business meeting, remember what a friend of mine told me: "Just because your phone rings doesn't mean you have to answer it." When you are in a meeting or having dinner with someone, if you start texting, those who are physically present with you will feel that you don't care what they have to say.

Be aware of the unspoken messages you send to people.

If you want to pursue this further for business purposes, follow the link in the Video Resources Section to "Phone Etiquette Training."[21]

# 51
## Are You Sabotaging Yourself with Email?

Most people don't think about their email when they start job hunting. As a result, they make poor impressions.

Talk about sending the wrong message! What's the first thing that comes to mind when you get an e-mail from hotbody@hotmail.com? Is this an egomaniac? Is this person a personal trainer? It sends all kinds of unprofessional thoughts through my head! On the other hand, a message from TomKnoley@TK.com appears professional and appropriate for someone looking for a new job. Need I ask which will impress a potential employer more? So, if you have a nutty e-mail address, change it to something more professional!

Most of the students with whom I work are always surprised that etiquette has anything to do with emails! But in business, email etiquette is essential. Here are some guidelines to follow.

- Subject line is to inform the purpose of the email. Keep it brief and relevant to content.
- Content should be on the formal side while always using a salutation, such as: "Dear Mr. King."
- Always use a surname rather than a first name until advised a first-name basis is acceptable.

This may be advised purely by a return signature.

- Don't shout! Using all UPPER-CASE LETTERS is considered CYBER SHOUTING!
- Remember no email is private! Discuss private matters in person or by phone.
- Always employ the 24-hour rule when sending an emotion-packed message. Cool down and be sure to re-read your message before sending.
- Always proofread all messages before sending.
- Use a signature line containing your first and last name, company (if applicable) and contact information at the end of every email. This is helpful to the recipient to contact you in other ways if necessary.

If interested in more information, use the link in the Video Resources Section for "Office Email Etiquette."[22]

# 52
# Texting While Walking Is a Recipe for Disaster

I was in a hurry. The line at Starbucks was out the door, and the guy in front of me took forever to decide on the three drinks and pastries he wanted to purchase. But I prevailed and got my venti extra shot latte. While I was carefully taking a sip as I exited the door, a guy with his face buried in his iPhone barreled into me as he furiously texted. The coffee scalded me and ruined my nicely pressed shirt. His apology? "Hey, Dude, watch where you're goin'!"

Excuse me? It took all my good manners to avoid an altercation. I felt like punching the guy. Now I'd have to go home, change my shirt and be even later than I expected for my morning appointment. But I bit my tongue, wiped myself off and changed shirts.

According to a Sept. 18, 2014 New York *Daily News* article, data from 100 hospitals showed that more than 1,500 pedestrians were treated in emergency rooms across the country for cell phone-related injuries in 2010. That's more than double the number treated in 2005. That number has doubled each year since 2006, according to a study conducted by Ohio State University.

The *Daily Mail* on Aug. 9 reported that a federal study revealed the number of pedestrian deaths and injuries has risen dramatically as a result of texting while walking. *Forbes* reported in mid-2012 that injuries from TWW range from facial fractures, nosebleeds and lacerations to foot and ankle injuries as a result of missing steps or walking into telephone poles at a result of handheld technology, not to mention collisions with other pedestrians or vehicles while crossing the street.

I shudder to think about that guy who ran into me walking into traffic or falling into a hole. And what about innocent pedestrians like me? I have a burn on my chest the size of Nevada.

Navigating the sidewalks of any major city can be as difficult as playing football at times. But when your opponents are walking while texting, they aren't watching where they're going. That can obviously make a two-block walk to Starbucks both maddening and life-threatening at the same time!

Let's gain more control over our increasingly electronic lives and stop acting like zombies with our BlackBerrys and iPhones replacing eye contact, handshakes and face-to-face conversation. Let's live in the present, be where we are and stop existing in cyber land. After all, what kind of an image are you creating with your nose in a cell phone most of the day?

### The Keys to Texting Etiquette

- For your own safety and that of others, don't text while walking or driving! The life you save really could be your own. And, do you really want to be responsible for harming others?
- Don't text during meetings or while having a meal or a conversation with someone in real time. Why? It's rude! It screams: The person on my cell phone is more important than you! Do you really want to send that message? (One of my recurring themes!)

178

- Use your cell phone for legitimate reasons, not to just "pass the time of day." If you must text, always tell others present with you that you have an important message to handle, and apologize and excuse yourself. Don't make a habit of this!
- Don't use texting as a means of communication for important issues. Text messages can be easily misunderstood, and you might end up miscommunicating important information.
- Use proper grammar and punctuation and keep your messages BRIEF. No more than two or three sentences. Messages become too unwieldy when they are longer.

Want more information about "Texting While Walking?" [23] follow the link in the Video Resources Section.

## 53
## How to Create an Effective Elevator Speech

An elevator speech sells an idea, promotes your business or markets you as an individual. It enhances your image. It's as essential as a business card and allows you to say who you are, what you are, what you do or are interested in doing, and how you can be a resource to your listener. Its purpose is to give people enough material to make them want to learn more about you. You can even use it at the beginning of an interview to give the other person enough info to make sense of you.

Here's an example. "Hi, my name is John Daly, and I teach etiquette, protocol and social skills, mostly to teens. What it does is turn their direction to a path of success. I'm teaching it in all the Santa Barbara Unified School District high schools, but I'd like to see this taught in every school in America. Might we discuss how this can make a difference in your school?"

According to Pepperdine University: Elevator speeches evolved during the early days of the Internet explosion when web development companies were courting venture capital. Finance firms were swamped with applications for money, and the companies that won the cash were often those with a simple pitch. The best were those that could explain a business proposition to the occupants of an elevator in the time it took them to ride to their floor. In other words, an elevator speech that worked was able to describe and sell an idea in 30 seconds or less. Today, if you don't have an elevator speech, people won't know what you really do.

To write a solid elevator speech, Pepperdine's Graziadio School of Business and Management recommends that you know your audience, know yourself, outline your talk and then finalize it.

### Know Your Audience

Before you do anything else, research your audience. An elevator speech needs to clearly target the people to whom you are going to speak. Generic pitches are doomed to failure.

### Know Yourself

If you want to convince anyone, you have to specifically define what you are offering, what problems you are capable of solving and what benefits you bring to prospective contacts or employers. So, answer the following questions:

- What are your key strengths?
- What adjectives come to mind to describe you?
- What are you trying to sell or let others know about you?
- Why are you interested in the company or industry the person represents?

### Outline Your Talk

Start with bullet points. No detail is necessary at this juncture. Just write notes to help you remember what you want to say. Address points like 1) Who am I? 2) What do I offer? 3) What problem can I solve or contributions can I make? 4) What do I want the listener to do after hearing my speech?

181

### Finalize the Speech

Take the outline and expand on your notes by writing out each section. Take each note you wrote and turn it into a sentence. Connect each sentence together with additional phrases to make them flow. Review what you have written and change long words into conversational language. Cut out unnecessary words. Try to target your speech to not exceed 90 words.

### Elevator Speech Examples

- Do you remember about 10 years ago when the space shuttle *Columbia* was destroyed on re-entry? It turns out the engineers tried to warn NASA about the danger. But the PowerPoint slides they used were a complete mess and no one understood the danger. That's what I do. I train people how to make sure their PowerPoint slides aren't a complete disaster. Students who attend my workshop can create slides that are 50 percent clearer and 50 percent more convincing, based on scores students give each other before and after the workshop.

I'm not sure if my training could work at your company. It really depends how much you use PowerPoint and what's at stake. Might we discuss it?

Use the link in the Video Resources Section for more information.[24]

~ ~ ~

- Hi, I'm John Doe, and I help businesses reduce their tax liability. Last year, after reviewing the books of one company, my suggestions reduced their federal and state taxes by 25 percent. I'm sure I could help your business save money as well. While some of my competitors charge an hourly rate, I use a flat fee so my clients know exactly what their costs will be. I am currently accepting new clients; may I send you some additional information?[24]

~ ~ ~

- It's so good to meet you. My name is Mary Smith. I have been helping women find their inner beauty for 15 years. The products I sell are only available through independent consultants and are not sold in stores. Our products pamper you and can make you look years younger. I have one client who is 67 years old and all her laugh lines disappeared after using our products. Can I interest you in a product brochure?[24]

# 54
# What You Can Learn from Madonna about Mastering Your Brand

I've been really focused on creating personal images and branding with my students of late. So, when I heard two radio personalities discussing Madonna, I was fascinated to learn that her dominance of the pop genre is the reason that virtually every performer (male and female) puts her on their Top 10 Greatest Talent list. Nowadays Lady Gaga and Beyonce get all of the attention, but Madonna was the original that these talented artists used for inspiration. She became a master at creating her brand and message and never lost sight of her goals.

This led me to do some research about Madonna and what drove her success. Here's what I discovered.

## Stand for Something

Madonna declared that she stood for freedom of expression, doing what she believed and pursuing her dreams. In business, marketers call "what you stand for" your Unique Selling Proposition. If you aren't living a defined message, you are dying a slow death. That's why Madonna has made defining and redefining her message her No. 1 priority for the last 20 years.

**Always Deliver**

Madonna believed in always holding up her end of the bargain and delivering on her contracts and commitments. She was born in Battle Creek, Michigan. Her good, old-fashioned work ethic came from her solidly Midwestern upbringing.

Look around and you'll see that every superstar (in whatever medium) has a relentless drive to keep delivering. They may not like the hours, but they know that the work is required.

**Be Clear About What You Want**

"A lot of people are afraid to say what they want. That's why they don't get what they want." — *Madonna*

Madonna's negotiating skills are legendary in the recording industry. She once was paid $5 million by Pepsi for a commercial the company never even ran. They got cold feet. No matter — Madonna still got paid. Madonna gets what she wants because she's been focused on exactly that from Day 1.

**Be a Work in Progress**

"I am my own experiment. I am my own work of art." —*Madonna*

Have fun with your brand. Once you've set your goal, have a blast getting there. Madonna is legendary for changing her image to fit the times and her own personal journey. Early on, critics tried to pigeonhole her as another big-hair pop act. "Like a Virgin" was her response. She's gone on to tweak her brand image for two decades.

You'll need to evolve, too. Your core will stay the same, but your tactics will need to change.

You may have to dial up some part of your personality to make a mark, or abandon a project entirely. Have the wisdom to know what's important for your brand. And while you're at it ...

### Don't Be Afraid to Stand Up for Your Beliefs

## "Better to live one year as a tiger than a hundred as a sheep." — *Madonna*

The secret to real respect is to absorb criticism, learn from it if that makes sense. Ignore the ones who aren't your people anyway, and keep moving forward. Remember, if everyone agrees with you, then you might not be saying anything worth talking about.

Conviction, creativity, and hard work, will never lose their appeal — much like Madonna.

## 55
## Gratitude Is the Right Attitude

The other day I was preparing a talk with one of my classes about gratitude and its importance. I was chatting on the phone with my friend and associate, Carol McKibben, and we were bouncing around our thoughts about why gratitude plays a large part in individual success stories.

As a result, Carol wrote the article below for her own blog, and, with her permission, I wanted to share it with some additional thoughts of my own.

### A Grateful Attitude Brings Success

We've all experienced it. After a dinner party, no note is sent. (Well, he was busy, and the dinner wasn't that elaborate.) The solicitous email gets no reply. (Again, he was busy, and didn't feel like chatting.) A driver gives way to him at a place where there is no clear priority; the courtesy isn't acknowledged.

A person holds a door; the recipient breezes on by with no word of thanks. On holiday, a couple gives the smallest and most worthless amount of money to those who have provided them services. The snotty teenager rails at the parent who scraped and saved for her.

The failure to give thanks beats at the heart of the sense of despair and gloom that is so pervasive in our society today.

Much of what plagues us can be tracked back to ingratitude. So, how can an attitude of gratitude bring about change while being unthankful can carry lethal results?

### Gratitude vs. Ingratitude

- Grateful people believe they have more than they deserve, while ungrateful folks believe they deserve more than they have and that the world owes them.
- A grateful person is loving and seeks to help others. An ungrateful person is bent on helping himself only, often willing to blame everyone else around him for his situation and sometimes prepared to get what he needs unlawfully or unethically.
- A grateful person feels a sense of fulfillment. Onc fillcd with ingratitude has a sense of emptiness.
- A thankful person is content. An ungrateful person is full of bitterness and discontent. Psychologists have reported that years of counseling with people who are chronically depressed, frustrated or emotionally unstable are those with little gratitude, regardless of the external circumstances that might appear to provide an explanation.
- A person filled with ingratitude sets himself or herself up for disappointment when others fail to perform according to his or her expectations. But a thankful person has no room for self-destructive emotions.

You might have heard that one of the characteristics that we can change is our attitude. Being grateful or ungrateful is a choice. Seeing the glass half-full or half-empty is a choice

I learned a long time ago that I enjoyed life a whole lot better when I was thankful for what I had in my life.

Rather than blame others, feel sorry for yourself or deciding to be disappointed with everything around you, change your attitude. Make a decision to be grateful for what you have.

You'll find that when you do, others will respect and like you better than someone who displays a selfish, uncaring attitude.

Try it. You'll see how success will find you if you do.

~ ~ ~

Carol is so correct. Gratitude is an attitude.

I know from personal experience. When I was a child, my mother raised my brother and me single-handedly.

At one point, we lost everything and lived in poverty. Rather than feeling sorry for ourselves, my diligent mother with her two young boys, pulled together to make a living.

Through hard work, my mother eventually was able to get a great job and get us out of the literal ghetto in which we lived. All the while, she taught us to be grateful for what we had.

That attitude stuck with me, and when I graduated from high school, I was determined to be successful, and I knew that an attitude of thankfulness to others would help me get there. I'd seen it work for my mother. I knew it would work for me, and it did beyond my wildest dreams — ending up with six businesses simultaneously and a lovely home for my wife and family.

I am grateful for it all and the attitude of gratitude that my mother taught me.

# INTERACTION

## Why Successful Interaction Matters

The art of conversation is indeed an art. Without the proper tools to be able to express your thoughts, feelings, and desires, you are at such a loss. I love what has happened with being able to text, email and tweet; however I have had the dangers of this wonderful advancement in technology get me into a lot of trouble. My Calendar is on line, my pictures are on line, my life, if you will, is on line, and it can so very easily be misconstrued when only reading or looking at a photo. The tabloids have been taking things out of context, exploiting them and making millions of dollars for years!

As you are aware, I spent many, many years in the event industry. I learned the importance of successful interaction during that time. Did you know that trying to describe a color in written words is next to impossible? Blue to my mind is far different that it is in your mind. "No, John, it's sky blue," they wrote. "Okay, I replied, "Was it cloudy that day or was the sun out?" Let me explain.

I remember doing a very large corporate event, entitled "Blue Agave," for a client years ago. We both wrote back and forth as our travel schedules just did not seem to jive so we could have a conversation. The day of the event arrived, and my client of many years walked into the room and said, "What is this? The colors are wrong." She had tons of printed material to go on all of the tables, and the blues clashed so badly it was hard to believe. Agave to me is a very gray blue, and to her it was what I call turquoise. Thank goodness we had done business for 25 + years and were able to make adjustments to the event that made it all work. We both learned a very large and expensive lesson that caused a great deal of stress for both of us. We never did an event again without finding the time to talk things out and overnight colors we were discussing. Sending them on the computer just does not work because every screen sees the color differently.

In addition to the myriad of miscommunication that can occur, the worst possible mistake with the written word is an attempt at humor, especially if you do not know the person with whom you are corresponding well. It can turn out to be very offensive rather than funny.

So, while email and texting is great for short answers, I never, ever make a final decision without talking to the person with whom I am dealing. Use the tools of the 21$^{st}$ century, but let's not forget the importance of the spoken word, either.

No matter how we interact – in writing or in conversation – it is critical that we assure that the other party understands so that all of our transactions can be successful. This last section emphasizes the importance of those interactions.

# 56
# Top 9 Conversation Etiquette Mistakes

Conversation blunders can hamper your business dealings, particularly everyday conversations. We have all said or done the wrong thing. The key is to learn from past mistakes and take a look at the most common conversation mistakes.

### No. 9 – One-upmanship

Want to alienate someone quickly? Try talking about your greatness in comparison to others. So, don't do this. Having a conversation with a client or an associate is not a competition. Avoid trying to "outdo" another person's good news or story. Give them their 15 minutes. There is plenty of time for you to have your time to shine.

### No. 8 – Not knowing your audience

What is appropriate conversation with a good friend is not always suitable for your boss or a client. Avoid rude jokes or topics about politics or religion with business-related conversation. When in doubt, stick to business topics.

### No. 7 – Changing the topic to suit your own interests

Don't force your preferred topics of conversation on others. Instead, let the conversation unfold naturally and contribute with relevant, on-topic information. Don't force a business conversation into a diatribe about your prowess on the basketball court or a political conversation about why everyone should vote a particular way.

### No. 6 – Checking your phone

It doesn't matter how important that next text or email is going to be. Checking your phone during a conversation is insulting to the person with whom you are conversing. Even though you live and breathe on everything that comes across on your phone, forget about it! When you pay more attention to your phone than the conversation you are having with the person in front of you, you are saying, "Hey, my phone messages are more important than you." (Have I stressed this enough and made my point in this book yet?) If you are with a client, that might just be the "kiss of death."

### No. 5 – Cursing

We've all done it. Sometimes, for the lack of a more appropriate word, we use profanity to enhance the conversation. If you are with your friends, the occasional use is not a big deal. But in business, it is unprofessional. If you want to get ahead in business, learn to express yourself without cursing.

### No. 4 – Not introducing participants

Proper introductions are imperative in business. It is inexcusable to not make them. There is nothing worse than letting someone sit quietly being ignored. You can get away with the old "I am so sorry. This is …" one time. Being a repeat offender is punishable by being sentenced to "no man's land."

### No. 3 – Looking over the other person's shoulder

It is not always easy to stay focused and totally engaged during an entire conversation. Maybe the conversation has dwindled down to the end, and you are thinking about the next item on your "to-do" list. Doesn't matter! Be respectful and keep your eyes on your companion. Resist the urge to look over the shoulder of your companion, even if Oprah Winfrey just walked through the door.

### No. 2 – Monopolizing the conversation

One of the most common conversation etiquette mistakes is monopolizing the conversation. It is uncomfortable for everyone involved. One-sided conversations are boring and make you appear to be an egomaniac. One of the best qualities you can have is your ability to listen and learn from others. Keep that in mind when you are tempted to try to control a conversation.

### No. 1 – Interrupting

Everyone makes this mistake. It is very common. It is also rude and disrespectful. It clearly lets your conversation partner know that you have no real interest in what he/she has to say. So how can you avoid it? Easy! As in No. 2, listen. And don't go blocking out what the other person is saying by thinking about what you are going to say next. Once you do, you won't be able to stop from blurting it out, defeating the purpose of listening to what the other person has to say. This is critical in a business conversation with a client or associate. You need to learn what the other party wants in order to have a meaningful business relationship.

### More Conversation Etiquette

To watch the video on conversation etiquette[25], follow the link in the Video Resources section.

# 57
# Conflict Resolution – Part 1 – How to Solve Disputes

Conflict happens. Different people with different goals and needs get into disputes that often result in intense personal animosity. On the other hand, disputes can often lead to personal and professional growth if they are resolved effectively.

Often, disputes are created by underlying problems, so look at them as an opportunity to solve the more deep-seated issues that create conflict. In addition, according to MindTools, if conflict is resolved effectively it can create:

- **Increased understanding:** The discussion to resolve conflict expands people's awareness of the situation, giving them an insight into how they can achieve their own goals without undermining those of other people.
- **Increased group cohesion:** When conflict is resolved effectively, team members can develop stronger mutual respect and a renewed faith in their ability to work together.
- **Improved self-knowledge:** Conflict pushes individuals to examine their goals in close detail, helping them understand the things that

197

are most important to them, sharpening their focus and enhancing their effectiveness.

If conflict is *not* handled effectively, the outcome can be very damaging, dissolving into personal dislike, a breakdown in teamwork and wasted talent when people disengage from their work. This becomes a vicious downward spiral of negativity.

To prevent this from happening, you need to understand two theories behind effective conflict resolution.

### The Theory of Conflict Styles

In the 1970s, Kenneth Thomas and Ralph Kilmann developed the Thomas-Kilmann Conflict Mode Instrument (TKI) to help identify which style of conflict resolution you tend toward.

- **Competitive Style:** People who tend toward this style take a firm stand and know what they want. They usually operate from a position of power (position, rank, expertise or persuasive ability). This style is useful when there is an emergency and a quick decision needs to be made; when the decision is unpopular; or when defending against someone who is trying to exploit the situation selfishly. However, it can leave people feeling bruised, unsatisfied and resentful when used in less urgent situations.

- **Collaborative Style:** People with this style try to meet the needs of all people involved. These people can be highly assertive but, unlike the competitor, they cooperate effectively and acknowledge that everyone is important. This style is useful when you need to bring together a variety of viewpoints to get the best solution; when there have been previous conflicts in the group; or when the situation is too important for a simple trade-off.

- **Compromising Style:** People who prefer this style try to find a solution that will at least partially satisfy everyone. Everyone is expected to give up something, and the compromiser also expects to relinquish something. Compromise is useful when the cost of conflict is higher than the cost of losing ground, when equal strength opponents are at a standstill and when there is a deadline looming.
- **Accommodating Style:** This style indicates a willingness to meet the needs of others at the expense of the person's own needs. The accommodator often knows when to give in to others, but can be persuaded to surrender a position even when it is not warranted. This person is not assertive but is highly cooperative. Accommodation is appropriate when the issues matter more to the other party, when peace is more valuable than winning, or when you want to be in a position to collect on this "favor" you gave. People may not return favors, however, and overall this approach is unlikely to give the best outcomes.
- **Avoiding Style:** People tending toward this style seek to evade the conflict entirely. This style is typified by delegating controversial decisions, accepting default decisions and not wanting to hurt anyone's feelings. It can be appropriate when victory is impossible, when the controversy is trivial or when someone else is in a better position to solve the problem. In many situations, however, this is a weak and ineffective approach to take.

Once you understand the different styles, you can use them to think about the most appropriate approach (or combination of approaches) for the situation. You can also think about your own instinctive approach, and learn how you need to change this if necessary. Ideally you can adopt an approach that meets the situation, resolves the problem, respects people's legitimate interests and mends damaged working relationships.

**The Theory of the "Interest-Based Relational Approach"**

The second theory respects individual differences while helping people avoid becoming too entrenched in a fixed position.

In resolving conflict using this approach, you follow these rules:

- **Make sure that good relationships are the first priority:** Be calm and try to build mutual respect. Be courteous to one another and remain constructive under pressure.
- **Keep people and problems separate:** Recognize that often the other person is not just "being difficult" — but that real and valid differences can lie behind conflictive positions. By separating the problem from the person, real issues can be debated without damaging working relationships.
- **Pay attention to the interests that are being presented:** By listening carefully, you'll most likely understand why the person is adopting his or her position.
- **Listen first; talk second:** It's imperative to understand where the other person is coming from before defending your own position.
- **Set out the "Facts":** Agree and establish the objective, observable elements that will have an impact on the decision.

- **Explore options together:** Be open to the idea that a third position may exist, and that you can get to this idea jointly.

By following these rules, you can often keep contentious discussions positive and constructive. This helps to prevent the antagonism and dislike that so often causes conflict to spin out of control.

In the next Chapter, I'll discuss using these tools to resolve conflict.

# 58
## Conflict Resolution – Part 2 - How to Solve Disputes

Now that I've outlined the theories of Conflict Styles and the Interest-Based Relationship Approach, a starting point to deal with conflict is to identify your own overriding conflict style and that of your team and your organization.

Over time, people's conflict management styles tend to mesh, and a "right" way to solve conflict emerges. However, make sure that people understand that different styles may suit different situations. Always consider the circumstances and the style that may be appropriate.

Then use the process below to resolve the conflict:

### Step One: Set the Scene
If appropriate to the situation, agree to the rules of the Interest-Based Relationship Approach (or at least consider using the approach yourself.) Make sure people understand that the conflict may be a mutual problem, which may be best resolved through discussion and negotiation rather than through raw aggression.

If you are involved in the conflict, emphasize the fact that you are presenting your perception of the problem. Use active listening skills (see the link in the References Section) to ensure you hear and understand the positions and perceptions of others.

- Restate.
- Paraphrase.
- Summarize.

And make sure that when you talk, you're using an adult, assertive approach (see the link in the Reference Section) rather than a submissive or aggressive style.

### Step Two: Gather Information

This step helps you get to the underlying interests, needs and concerns. Ask for the other person's viewpoint and confirm that you respect his or her opinion and need his or her cooperation to solve the problem. Try to understand his or her motivations and goals, and see how your actions may be affecting these.

Also, try to understand the conflict in objective terms: Is it affecting work performance? Damaging the delivery to the client? Disrupting team work? Hampering decision-making? Be sure to focus on work issues and leave personalities out of the discussion.

- Listen with empathy and see the conflict from the other person's point of view.
- Identify issues clearly and concisely.
- Use "I" statements.
- Remain flexible.
- Clarify feelings.

### Step Three: Agree on the Problem

This sounds obvious, but often different underlying needs, interests and goals can cause people to perceive problems differently. You'll need to agree upon the problems that you are trying to solve before you'll find a mutually acceptable solution.

Sometimes different people will see different but interlocking problems — if you can't reach a common perception of the problem, then at the very least, you need to understand what the other person sees as the problem.

### Step Four: Brainstorm Possible Solutions
If everyone is going to feel satisfied with the resolution, everyone must have fair input in generating solutions. Brainstorm possible solutions, and be open to all ideas, including ones you never considered before.

### Step Five: Negotiate a Solution
By this stage, the conflict may be resolved: Both sides may better understand the position of the other, and a mutually satisfactory solution may be clear to all.

However, you may also have uncovered real differences between your positions. This is where a technique like win-win negotiation (see the link in the Reference Section) can be useful to find a solution that hopefully satisfies everyone.

There are three guiding principles here:
- Be Calm
- Be Patient
- Have Respect

### Key Takeaways
Conflict in the workplace can be incredibly destructive to good teamwork.

Managed in the wrong way, real and legitimate differences between people can quickly spiral out of control, resulting in damaging situations in which cooperation breaks down and the team's mission is threatened. This is particularly the case where the wrong approaches to conflict resolution are used.

To solve these situations, it helps to take a positive approach to conflict resolution. This means discussion is courteous and non-confrontational, and the focus is on issues rather than on individuals. If this is done and if people listen carefully and explore facts, issues and possible solutions properly, conflict can often be resolved effectively.

## 59
## How to Bond with Your Boss

*Jeanne Nelson, an admired associate of mine, recently wrote an article I wanted to share with you. I think you will find it has extremely valuable information.*

~ ~ ~

The key to a positive work experience is forging a great — or at least good — relationship with your boss. That might be a challenge with some bosses (think Miranda in *The Devil Wears Prada*), but when you're hired, this becomes your No. 1 Priority. For the time that you report to a particular manager, that person holds your career with the company in his or her hands. There are exceptions, but generally speaking, that's the rule.

As a brand-new hire, you have a specific relationship with your boss, which is different from that of transferring in from another department as a more experienced employee. Therefore, you have some things to prove to earn your new manager's trust and respect. You have a good start, of course; your manager liked you enough to hire you! And, your ability to perform optimally will depend on your manager's continued liking for you! Thus, knowing how to "manage up" is essential to solidify that relationship.

## What is Managing Up?

Managing up is the handling of your relationship with your boss. It's not managing your boss; she or he will be the one who will be doing the managing — of you. Getting that straight will be fundamental to your strategy, which should include focusing on fulfilling the needs and requirements of your manager in order to (1) make his or her star shine even brighter and (2) elevate your business unit to (even higher) prominence.

What managing up isn't is sucking up, which is repugnant and self-serving. Nor is it manipulation or duplicity to gain your own ends. Remember, you want to be authentic, ethical and trustworthy, and demonstrate your integrity in everything you do.

By doing what you were hired to do — and by outperforming in the execution of those responsibilities — you will increase the odds of gaining the appreciation and admiration of your boss and attract the attention of other managers. These are the prerequisites to career advancement.

To help you place your relationship with your new boss in the proper perspective and achieve a productive and enjoyable rapport, following are some tips on how to "manage up":

### Loyalty

Your boss wants to be assured that she has your loyalty. Never talk negatively about her or betray confidences to anyone. Don't go around her or over her head. Support her in public, disagree with her in private. Bring issues to her attention even if others hesitate to do so, especially if doing so will protect or forewarn her of something she should address. Keep her confidences. Have her back.

### Dependability

Do your job. Show up for work on or before your scheduled start time, or whenever you're needed. Meet or exceed deadlines. Anticipate your boss' needs and take action. Don't let him down. Be true to your word. Make sure your work is accurate and that you carry out your responsibilities with impeccable care.

By focusing on completing your currently assigned tasks better than anyone before you, your boss will be more receptive to promoting you or giving you that plum assignment.

Whatever keeps your boss up at night, don't let it have anything to do with your dependability. Become the rock (star) upon which he depends.

### Focus

Take a page from the executive assistant's playbook: focus on the needs of your boss and her department. Make sure that her priorities are your priorities. Find out how you can make her job easier. Ask questions. Be observant about your boss' likes and dislikes. What pushes her buttons? What impresses her? What lightens her mood? Is she an early bird? How does she work, and how does she want you to tackle assignments?

By tying her needs and desires to your job performance, you will increase your value and make yourself close to indispensable.

### Communication

Is your boss a big-picture or fine-detail communicator? Does he want "just the facts, ma'am" or does he want to be filled in on every point? Does he prefer face-to-face briefings or email summaries? Learn and adapt to avoid frustration and maintain productive communications. Then, discuss issues, ask questions, present ideas and collaborate thoroughly on projects, as appropriate. When advising your boss of a problem, always have a suggested solution, and when proposing an idea, always include supporting data.

## ROAR

Become Results Oriented And Relevant (ROAR). Often when you're in a salaried position you can get bogged down in becoming process oriented. This is usually due to the rules and protocols you must follow in performing your job.

But this is precisely the reason the concept of "thinking of out the box" came into fashion. When you repeatedly run into obstacles in completing a particular task or assignment in a reasonable period or meeting deadlines without loose ends to be tied up, it's time to be creative. That means finding a new way to achieve the results your boss wants.

How many times have I heard my bosses over the years say to me, "I don't care how you do this; just get it done!" Sometimes you'll be able to see how a process can be improved in order to achieve results faster. Of course, when you're tinkering with a process you must ensure that quality and accuracy are not sacrificed; such setbacks can cause delays in achieving results, not to mention embarrassment and reputational loss.

Therefore, to be a leader and innovator rather than a paper pusher means constantly looking for ways to improve processes to achieve better and faster results. And, achieving better and faster results on a regular basis is a major way to strengthen the bond between you and your boss, whether those results are routine or extraordinary, small or large.

### Boss Man vs. Boss Lady

Are there differences between male and female bosses? Studies over the years have revealed that all things being equal, gender does not play a big role in the ability to manage. The key is "all things being equal," which, of course, they are not, and never have been.

The more accurate indication of a boss' approach to managing has more to do with the environment and level of respect and support from his or her higher ups and colleagues.

In general, if a female manager is alone in a sea of male managers, she might be more threatened by other women who aspire to leadership roles because she knows that she's occupying the token spot that will be accorded to a woman.

One only has to look at the percentages of female *Fortune 500* CEOs, women in Congress and female U.S. presidents to understand the feelings of female managers in a male-dominated environment.

In such a case, it's important to know that loyalty is at the top of the list of qualities a female boss seeks in her subordinates. On the other hand, a female boss who's in a field, company or department that's dominated by women might be inclined to have a more relaxed management style.

There is, of course, the perception, promulgated through the ages by the media and those who have been uninformed or bigoted, that a woman is not as equipped as a man to manage, and that when a woman assumes a leadership role she breaches her stereotypic feminine nature. Enlightened professionals know that is horsefeathers, but the fallacy persists.

Having both reported to women and been a manager myself I can assure you that working for a boss lady can be an enjoyable and rewarding experience!

## 60
## How to Gain Employee Commitment

Are you part of a business setting in which employees don't follow directions well? Are you a boss or team leader frustrated by employees who don't make your assignments happen?

Case in point: A business owner I know held a large meeting with his employees. At the end of the meeting, he invited everyone to dinner to thank them for their hard work. Unfortunately, he left the office and never told his employees where to go for dinner. He assumed they knew where to go.

To try to guess where he meant, his employees went to several places the boss usually goes. However, he wasn't there.

They all ended up frustrated and angry with the boss, while he sat in the restaurant waiting for them and thinking they blew him off. He became angry, and everyone went home upset. The moral of the story: If you do not tell people where you want them to go, you can't expect them to get there.

To obtain employee commitment and follow-through, managers must communicate to their team why they need to do things instead of what they should do.

Instructing employees on what to do generally results in their trying to follow your directions without understanding the mission. In addition, they may not even be aware that they are going in the wrong direction, since all they're doing is following instructions.

### The Solution — Provide Goals and Objectives

It is much easier to have your team achieve your goals and objectives if you coach them on why they are supposed to do certain tasks. Tell them your goals and objectives for specific tasks.

It makes it so much easier for employees to figure out what to do to get there because they are actually closer to the action. They most likely will find better ways to do things rather than you having to try to micromanage them with blow-by-blow instructions.

You will build a feeling of trust and commitment if you let them devise how to get things done. Even if they require guidance on what to do, it will be based on a specific objective.

Finally, it is imperative that companies provide and emphasize their mission statements to employees. A mission statement is at the core of any business' existence. It should be on the walls, in the employee manual and the purpose of every goal and objective.

So, to get employee commitment and meaningful action, management must always direct employees as to *why* things have to be done rather than just what employees *should* do.

Whether you are management or part of the employee pool, having this knowledge will help you manage down or up. That's right, managers can learn from employees with all the right interaction.

# 61
## How to Provide Constructive Criticism

Not long ago, I had the opportunity to observe a manager handing out criticism to his team members. What I noticed is that the criticism was less "constructive" and more "destructive." This inspired me to come up with a list of tips for anyone in a position to provide positive feedback that is needed and wanted.

**First, consider your attitude about the person to be critiqued.** Be honest. If you have any negative thoughts about this person, it isn't appropriate for you to offer him or her advice.

**Begin and close with a compliment.** At the start, always find something positive to say. This will make the team member feel good about the advice you are providing. Close with another compliment. This will prevent the person from feeling like a failure or that you are angry.

**Make eye contact with the person you are critiquing.** This tells the person you are being honest and sincere. Really focus on the person. Don't offer suggestions over your shoulder, or while you are busy multitasking.

**Take care with your tone of voice.** This communicates more than your words. If your voice is harsh, has an edge or you are flippant with them, criticism will be harder for them to swallow from you.

213

**Try not to say anything that is hurtful.** Rather than trying to be harsh and "in command," be gentle. For instance, say something like, "I really like the way you speak to your supervisor. Your team members would really respond well to you if you spoke to them the same way."

**Talk about the behavior, not the person.** Don't be insulting. Don't make your criticism personal. Focus on the fact that providing feedback is a way to illustrate a person's improvement. Don't say, "You are a terrible example for other people." Rather, "You are your team's role model. Your behavior is teaching them the incorrect way to lead others."

**If possible, deliver criticism light-heartedly.** This "lifts the air around both of you." It makes what you have to say more positive. Dr. Barton Goldsmith, a speaker and business consultant, affirms that "Humor doesn't diminish the seriousness of the feedback you are giving. It actually helps the person receiving the direction to open up and take it in."

**Don't nag. Don't hold a grudge.** Once you have offered constructive criticism, let it go. The person will either accept your advice or ignore it. She or he will have to suffer the consequences if the choice is to ignore helpful advice. Never give criticism in front of others or at a bad time. Provide criticism in private. When someone is hungry or tired, he or she may not be in the best frame of mind to absorb your advice. So choose the time and place wisely to assure the best possible outcome for offering your advice.

Dr. Goldsmith, who presents to companies, associations and leaders worldwide, offers that these are the best tools to make teams strong. He feels that knowing how to give feedback and constructive criticism in a way that it is taken in and learned from may be a leader's greatest tool for effective team building.

# 62
# Conversation as an Art Form

Have you heard the expression: "Conversation is a lost art?"

In this era of technology, it's easy to see how that expression could become reality. So many people today would rather text or email as opposed to having a real conversation.

But, let's face it; in the day-to-day of the business world, you'll be a standout if you know how to carry on a healthy conversation. What do I mean by "healthy?"

**First, it's more important that you *listen* rather than talk.** Most people's favorite topic is themselves. So when you meet someone new, ask them not only what they do but ask what makes the job interesting, or difficult or challenging. Find out the outlook for that profession. Appear interested by looking into the person's eyes and shaking your head in agreement when appropriate.

**When you know you are going to meet new people, be prepared.** If you are going to a business social affair, and you will be meeting with some prospective clients there, read up on their companies. Ask questions that you've gleaned from your research, such as, "I see the company is expanding operations. Tell me how that affects you."

**Avoid politics, sex or religion.** These can be volatile topics. Better yet try to direct the conversation to topics of

215

interest to the group with which you are seated or with whom you find yourself. For me, going to a dinner with my old event professional buddies means I will be talking events. But going to a Santa Barbara Partners in Education event will focus my conversation on students.

**Watch the body language of others when you are talking.** After you've talked for several minutes, if you notice that no one has asked questions, made comments or that they appear somewhat bored, ask a question that will induce another in the group to take over the conversation.

**Never interrupt another.** Never interrupt someone in midsentence. Always wait until the person who has the floor stops talking. Never ask someone if they have finished. That really comes across as rude. Avoid using such phrases as "By the way" or "Your story reminds me of ..." If you do, you are interrupting the other person's discussion and sending it off in another direction. You will appear interested only in what you have to say.

If you are the person interrupted, the best thing to do is just be quiet. Don't try to re-introduce your train of thought later unless you are asked to do so. Let another person in the group ask you to continue your story. If you don't get that request, perhaps you should take that as your clue that no one was really interested!

**Avoid foot-in-mouth disease.** The best remedy is to think before you speak. Avoid creating awkward situations like mentioning someone else's illness in front of a friend whose parent just passed away. Don't make judgmental statements. For instance, instead of saying "Jane Smith is an idiot." Say, "Have you been to Jane Smith's new restaurant?"

**Don't share too much information.** Don't be the person who pours out your life story to strangers. That reeks of desperation and makes people want to retreat as soon as possible. It's just not cool. Don't do it. While you are at it, don't "nose" into others' personal lives. Always remember to respect others' privacy. If you want to get to know a person a bit better, offer "a little" about yourself and then see if the other person reciprocates. If not, change the subject.

**When in a group, don't just focus on one person.** If you are in a group where you particularly gravitate to one person, don't freeze out the others. You freeze out others by selecting topics of no interest or knowledge to the others in the group. If you do this, and only the one person engages and everyone else disengages, that should be your clue to bring up subjects that everyone can enjoy.

**Never say "Stop me if I've told you this story before ..."** No one will. All you are doing is prolonging the many times people have heard a familiar story over and over. If you think they might have heard it, avoid it.

**Never say "Am I boring you?"** Another one no one will ever say "yes" to. This is the time to really watch body language and facial expressions. If they look bored, they probably are. Don't go there.

**Be Natural.** You can use these rules as a guideline, not a checklist. Be yourself. Let your personality shine through. Never pretend to be someone you are not. Being polite doesn't mean being phony.

# 63
# When an Audience Isn't Engaged

What if you have to make a presentation? Let's look at the following scenario.

It has been a busy conference. The participants are close-knit professionals and love to share their ideas and enthusiasm. They are gathered together in a large meeting room to listen to a colleague who is not a professional speaker.

At the onset, instead of giving the presenter their full attention, audience members are busy sharing and chatting to the point of being rude. What's the speaker to do? What should the event manager do?

I've seen several suggestions in various discussion groups to which I belong. Everything from 1) Stop the speech and ask everyone to pay attention, to 2) Quietly go about the room politely asking audience members to please stop talking and listen, to 3) Ignore it and hope it will go away!

I don't recommend Nos. 2 and 3. No. 1 is an option. If the speaker suddenly gets quiet and just waits, people will notice and become silent as well.

I know one speaker who, when faced with an inattentive audience, simply stopped talking and raised her arm straight up in the air. This is an old "Girl Scout camp" trick that Beth Cooper-Zobott, director of Conference Services at Equity Residential, suggests. As a member of a noisy audience, she once just raised her arm and everyone followed suit and got quiet! She recommends that anyone who does speaking should put this idea in the "trainer/speaker tool belt" and use it as a part of a "canned" segue into the presentation by sharing a personal anecdote to warm up the audience.

The key here isn't to chastise those in the audience who weren't speaking, so as not to lump them in with those who were being discourteous, and to handle the situation smoothly no matter our level of frustration. For example, she says, a room is noisy/chatty. I begin, and chatting continues. I raise my hand straight in the air. Those in the room notice and grow silent. I thank the room and say conversationally, "Raising your hand to focus a group's attention is something I learned when I was about 7, when I was a Brownie Scout and a member of Mrs. Houseman's Troop 13 in Elgin, Illinois. By a show of hands, who among us was in Girl Scouts or Boy Scouts? For some of us, that may have been our first experience as a part of a team of leaders. Today, we're all leaders in our industry and the leadership issue we'll be talking about today is ..."

If you have ever been a part of this situation and would like advice on how to resolve it, let's back up and take a look at how this should have been handled from the planning stages. If you ever have to sit on a planning committee, provide education for a local or national association or a meeting, these are good tips to follow.

- Particularly when working with a nonprofessional speaker, event management should send the presenter a list of techniques to effectively engage an audience. A Google search will unveil a plethora of articles to prepare presenters to engage an audience. Always send the list to the presenter in an upbeat manner that lets him or her know that you are available to help make preparation easy.

- Plan with the speaker to have staff on hand with wireless microphones (if it is going to be a large audience) to start with an interactive session right out of the gate. If audience members realize that the speaker might call on them to answer a question, they will get immediately focused. This is particularly useful with a novice speaker and an audience that historically likes to socialize. It's always good to have a few "plants" in the audience to get the ball rolling.

- The person introducing the speaker should make some general housekeeping announcements, such as "turn off your cell phones" and other information of note and then call the session to "order" indicating full attention.

- If you ever have to make a presentation and are like 99 percent of the population (who face it with dread), simply start your talk with a confession that you are nervous. Why? It will elicit compassion from the audience and help you feel more in control.

- Brian Monahan of Prestige AV & Creative Services suggests that participants receive a set of "Ground Rules" for attending meetings. They are:
  o Respect the forum with decorum.
  o Remove yourself from the room if you cannot honor the presenter/attendees with your attention.
  o Be empowered to request others to honor the ground rules of the event.
  o Ask yourself how you would want to be treated if given the same stage, and do that.
  o Don't attend if you cannot honor these simple rules.

Everyone I've spoken with about this topic agrees that it has always been an ongoing challenge. When you are faced with either planning, participating or serving as a presenter, keep these simple tricks in mind to keep things on track.

For more information, follow the link in the Video Resources Section for "How to Keep Your Audience's attention."[26]

# 64
# How to Deal with Unwanted Calls

We've talked about how not to use your phone, or how to tame an angry caller. But how do we handle a particular annoyance. We all get them ... unwanted phone calls. Whether it's from a telemarketer, a chatty relative who just won't get off the phone, or calls from a persistent acquaintance or even a stalker!

Everyone's first reaction is to just rudely cut them off. Not a good idea. This world has far too much rudeness in it, and there are kinder ways to handle them.

Fortunately, with today's technology, Caller ID allows us to identify the caller. That way, we can ignore the call when we need to and return it when it's more convenient for us.

If ignoring the call isn't an option or you don't know who is calling, here are some ways to deal with unwanted phone calls.

### Telemarketers

If you're like me, you'll see an unknown number, and, out of curiosity you answer the phone. Unfortunately, it's a telemarketer who immediately begins his sales pitch. You so wish you'd let it go to voicemail!

In these situations, plenty of people are tempted to start cursing and yelling, but that's the worst way to handle things.

Remember, a telemarketer is just doing his job. No need for you to be impolite or use profanity. Just politely wait for the person to catch his breath and say, "I'm sorry, but I'm not interested." Then hang up.

To avoid getting more of these calls in the future, register your telephone number with the National Do Not Call Registry.

### Super Chatty Cathy

Everyone has experienced telephone conversations with another person who just won't stop talking or end the phone call. Polite hints like "hmmm" or "I see" clearly illustrate our lack of interest. Chatty Cathy just keeps on talking anyway. We're thinking of a way to politely end the conversation and not disrespect or hurt the other person's feelings. Chatty Cathy is oblivious to it all.

When this happens, and you get a call from Chatty Cathy, be prepared to end the conversation before it gets started. Say: "Hi, I just wanted to answer and say hello, but I really don't have time to talk right now. May I call you back?" If you let the other person launch into conversation, you won't have a chance to end it!

### Unwanted Business Associates

One of my friends complained to me about constant, unwanted calls from a former business associate and monthly voice mail messages that she feels compelled to return. She's tried putting him off to no avail. The caller's interest is purely business, and he is merely diligent in making calls to ensure that he stays in touch with his network of contacts.

She asked me if it would be rude not to call him back. My response: yes, the calls should be returned; but she need not be the one to return them. Instead, she should assign that task to a secretary, assistant, intern or a junior officer who can return his calls in a polite but perfunctory manner. That avoids burning bridges, which is never a good idea.

We all run into pesky associates who are harmless but try to take up our time. It's part of business to just cope with them. Having someone else return the calls (wherever possible) will avoid a drain on your time.

### The Stalker

In extreme situations, unwanted calls may actually be harassment. Whether an angry friend, total stranger or past relationship, take these types of calls seriously. Try to avoid answering the calls, and do not respond to harassment. Call your phone company and notify them of the calls. They may be able to prevent the number from calling you.

If the harassment doesn't stop or is taking the form of threats, keep a log of all harassing calls and save any voicemail messages. Keeping a record of these calls will allow you to produce voicemail messages for the authorities.

Notify law enforcement to file a report. The police should step in and take action to stop the stalker. You may also need to change your phone number.

While unwanted phone calls can be a drain on your time and energy, you need to weigh each one and make sure that you handle them with kindness and respect. In the case of harassing phone calls, be sure that your first priority is your own safety.

## 65
## How to Become a Savvy Emailer

Most of us will recognize a situation in which we receive an email from an associate or colleague that leaves us with multiple questions. The email is vague, has a subject line like "I have a question …" and isn't clear about what is being asked of you.

Let's face it: technology has made us a bit lazy. We're so obsessed with the speed with which we can contact others and get quick answers that being clear, polite and considerate of the recipient falls by the wayside.

Don't get me wrong. I'm all for getting a lot more done in a day than it used to take. Email, Twitter and even texting have clear benefits. But the 140 characters used for Twitter isn't always the best way to handle an email, particularly where business is concerned.

Most offices prefer that their employees communicate in a highly professional manner. Let's examine some of my recommendations for extending consideration and proper courtesy to clients and co-workers alike.

- Before you even write an email, decide whether what you have to say would be better delivered by a telephone call or a face-to-face meeting. Email should never be used to avoid a difficult situation or a problem that needs to be discussed.

- Be concise (not 140 characters) but cover the topic in an efficient manner.
- Use proper grammar and punctuation.
- Because people are busy, they tend to scan emails. So always put the most important information in the first paragraph.
- When replying, always answer all questions thoroughly to avoid back and forth conversation. I can't tell you how many times I've had to ask for clarification for both questions and responses sent to me.
- Re-read your entire email before sending it. Check your grammar, spelling and thoroughness. See if you can avoid answering in a convoluted manner. Make it thorough but succinct.
- Structurally, set your email up like a business letter. That means it should have an introductory sentence and acceptable paragraph lengths.
- Avoid abbreviations and emoticons. Save them for text messaging to a friend.
- Don't shout at the addressee. In other words, don't write in all capital letters. And, don't use all lowercase text.
- Only use the "highly important" options when what you are sending *is* urgent or a priority. If you mark everything as such, people will stop believing you!
- Make sure that your subject lines are very specific.
- Use a signature block on all correspondence so the person to whom you are writing will have all your contact information, including your

full name, title, company name, phone number, email address and company Web site address. This makes finding your information much easier for the person receiving the message.

- Create a distribution mailing list so that the name of the list will appear in the "to" field instead of the names of everyone receiving the list.
- Don't overload people. Don't "Reply to All" if you only need to respond to the sender.
- Write separate emails for separate topics.
- Don't request read or delivery receipts for every email.
- Never forward chain letters, jokes or nonbusiness email. Most employers prefer that you not do so.
- Don't forward confidential information out of respect for the sender.
- Never forward an attachment without the original sender's permission.

When you review these, you'll realize you are only making it easier for the addressee to understand your needs and respond accordingly. No matter whether you are sending an email or replying to one, these rules apply.

If you are interested in watching a video on how to write a proper email[27], follow the link in the Video Resources Section.

# 66
# How to Avoid Awkward Introductions

I'm willing to bet that the following situation has happened to you. One of your friends introduces you to another person. You stick out your hand, smile, look the person in the eye and say, "Nice to meet you." Then, the dreaded words come out of a disappointed expression on the other's face. "We've met, *twice*."

How do you recover? Stay calm and use something like, "Of course! Please forgive my memory lapse. It's great to see you again." Or, apologize and use a bit of humor. "I remember children's and dog's names, but I'm obviously not great with adults!"

Often I will know someone and completely draw a blank — even if I know them well. Call it an age thing if you like, but it is still difficult.

To avoid that situation ever happening again, consider helping people out. For instance, if you are standing with a group and someone you know approaches, be the first to stick out your hand and greet him or her. I always ask everyone if they've met each other. If not, I ask them to please introduce themselves.

While they are doing that I try to listen for their names yet again. This is always good if you can't remember everyone's full names in the group. Look at it as helping others out.

Of course, if everyone is wearing name tags on his or her right shoulder, that will solve the problem. But that's isn't always the case. And, it's sometimes difficult to scramble to look at a name tag when the lighting is less than desirable at a gathering.

If you do know the person who approaches you well, be sure that everyone is properly introduced. If you take the lead and introduce others in the group, this will also give the newcomer a chance to voice who he or she has or has not already met.

Another potential hazard to avoid is approaching someone at a networking event and start talking to him or her as if you had been together the previous day. The person you've approached may have met you in the past; however, he or she may not remember your name. So, if you approach someone you see infrequently, always say, "Hi, Carol. It's John Daly. I am so happy to see you!"

I do a lot of speaking to all different types of groups and often people expect me to know them because they were in a seminar I taught. I am sorry to say that it is all a sea of faces while I am speaking. While I may be able to see a name tag and call someone by name, it is always important to introduce yourself again at the evening function when we see each other. A simple, "Hi, John, it's Jane here" works. And it makes all feel more comfortable when I say "Of course, Jane, you were in my seminar today."

Often seeing someone out of the normal context can throw a person. That's why you should always make a self-introduction, such as "Hi, John Daly here."

The key is to prevent an embarrassing situation for the other person and yourself. How?

- Always make sure everyone in your group gets a proper introduction. You can always ask,

"Carol, do you know Bob?" Never assume that everyone knows each other.

- When approaching someone, always say your full name, such as "Hi! John Daly here. Great to see you!" Don't ever assume that person will remember any or all of your name.
- If someone approaches you, and you don't remember his or her name, or that you met previously, just be honest and apologize. Use tasteful humor to let the person know that you aren't good at remembering everyone's names.

The bottom line in any embarrassing situation is to remember to be honest and polite. None of us are infallible. It's not comfortable to make another unhappy with us, but let your warmth and genuine interest in that person in that moment overcome any mistake in remembering his or her name or face.

# 67
## The ABCs of the Constant Interrupter

Do you have a friend, colleague, client or boss who constantly interrupts you when you are in the middle of a thought? Does that person "run away" with the topic you began or, even worse, take it in another direction than you intended? Does this convince you that it isn't worth communicating when that person is involved? The problem is that the relationship will suffer if you take this tact. You will withdraw from him or her and pretty much "disconnect" and feel resentment, even anger.

You can go negative, but *don't*. Instead shift your attitude and ask yourself if the person's behavior is intentional. Always look at any relationship with intention. Yes, sometimes people are frustratingly irritating while simultaneously being totally unaware. When there is no intention on their part, you should have more patience with them. So, rather than turning negative and being offended, look at why some people are chronic "interrupters."

Here's a list of *why* people interrupt formulated by Marion Grobb Finkelstein, the Communication Catalyst, an author, speaker and expert who teaches business and people to improve their lives with better communications.

### It May Be How They Process

Some people interrupt because it's how they process and interpret information. In their enthusiasm to show you they're on the same wavelength as you, they interrupt and ironically sabotage their very efforts to connect with you. It's not meant to be rude or disrespectful. Actually, quite to the contrary — it's often intended as a sign that they are actively engaged in what you're saying.

### It May Come From a Place of Service

If you are the type of communicator who requires long pauses between thoughts as you process information, you might unknowingly be inviting this interrupting behavior. Sometimes people interrupt thinking that a prolonged pause is an invitation to fill in the blank. Or they believe they are helping provide a service to find the words for what they see as you grappling. They fill in the blanks, the voids, the dead air with thoughts they believe you are trying to express.

### It May Be Time Pressures

Other times, people are just rushed and need to speed up the communication process and get on to the other million tasks that beckon them. Interrupting is their way, albeit ineffective, of keeping the conversation moving at breakneck speed. They are juggling so many balls and are so time-crunched they are oblivious as to how they are potentially damaging a relationship so they can run to the next urgent matter yelling for their attention.

### It May Be Anger or Frustration

If someone has tried several times to speak up and feels that they are not being heard, they may resort to interrupting. It's not right or necessarily effective. It is, however, a very human response, and we all do it from time to time. Ask yourself if this person is constantly interrupting you, or is it only when you're discussing certain volatile, emotional subjects? If he or she is angry or passionate about the subject being discussed, as frustrating as you being interrupted may be, it's less about you than it is about his or her need to be heard. It's not necessarily against you; it's for them.

**POINT: People Seldom Interrupt with the Specific Intent of Irritating You**

Once you understand that we're all different, it helps to build bridges between communication styles. If you're dealing with someone who interrupts, you might not be able to change his or her behavior, but you can sure change yours. If you find you're constantly being interrupted by all types of people, it might be *your* communication style that needs tweaking.

What can you do about that? Speak faster. Invite comments before you complete your thought, or ask the interrupter to give you a sec to finish what you were saying.

Finally, if the person who constantly interrupts you is unaware, take the time to sit down with him or her and diplomatically make him/her aware of the problem. Ask if the two of you can work on it together. That's way better than just letting the behavior get you down!

As Finkelstein says, "It all begins with how you think. Take responsibility for that piece and your role in the communication dance, and you'll be amazed at how you can change the dynamics between you and others."

# 68
# Relationships Can Be a Challenge at Any Age

I recently had coffee with a friend of mine, and he shared with me the details of an uncomfortable situation in his home.

His 86-year-old mother lives with him and his wife. She met and began dating an elderly gentleman from her church. He became very serious about her rather quickly. While all she wanted was a friend with whom to go out to eat, go to the movies and do some shopping, he had other ideas. After only a few dates, he wanted to marry her!

This went on for about six weeks, with him pushing for a commitment, and her holding him off at arms-length. Even counseling from their pastor didn't put the brakes on the elderly gentlemen. His attitude was: "I don't have all that much time, so I need to go for what I want."

Unfortunately, his behavior completely "turned off" my friend's mother. She came home after one of her outings with her "boyfriend" and asked for her son's help in "breaking up" with the gentleman. Her point was that they each had such opposing agendas that it would never work. She felt if she tried to do it alone that he would just ignore her and try to continue the relationship.

So, my friend called up the "boyfriend" and invited him to come over. He was present while his mother explained that because they wanted two separate outcomes in the relationship that it would not work out between them. When she told him she would not be available to go out with him any longer, the older man broke down and cried. My friend and his mother felt terrible.

But, that's where the real problem begins. His mother feels so badly about hurting her beau that she now won't go to church in fear of seeing him and hurting him even more.

My advice was simply to counsel his mother, letting her know that she did the right thing. I explained that it was not fair to either of them to continue a relationship that would only frustrate them both. Ultimately, it frees her old beau to pursue another who might be more open to the idea of marriage and a long-term relationship.

Hurting someone is never fun, but what's even more important is to respect the other person enough not to lead them on or let them suffer under any false delusions. Honesty is truly the best policy in any relationship. It's the only way to treat another person. If you try to do otherwise, it will only end in more hurt for both parties.

# 69
# How to Address an Envelope

Why have you positioned this in interaction, you might ask? Actually, when this was originally published, I took a lot of grief about it! Some said, "Any simpleton knows how to address an envelope, and what does it have to do with interaction and behavior? It's simple enough. Right? However a number of questions always arise in the ever-changing society in which we live.

I first started thinking about this topic when I received an envelope in the mail that disturbed me! The person had written my address with a fountain pen instead of the typical ballpoint, and much of the return address was smeared. A big blotch appeared in the upper left-hand corner.

This got me to thinking about general guidelines for addressing envelopes. Most of the time you can use the general rules of addressing an envelope, whether it is a thank-you note or a business letter. Actually, you wouldn't believe some of the crazy ways people have addressed envelopes to me. And what kind of impression do you think such faulty interaction makes on another? So bear with me. I'll bet there's one tidbit in this topic that will be helpful to you.

**Return Address**
In the upper left-hand corner, place the sender's name on the top line, the street address or post office box on the second line and the city, state and ZIP code on the third.

**Addressee's Information**
This detail goes in the center of the envelope. You put the name of the intended recipient on the top line, his or her street address on the next line, and the city, state and ZIP on the third. Exactly like you write the sender's information. You may need a fourth line for the name of the company or unit number for an apartment or suite. But remember to put a space after the city name, use the two-letter capitalized abbreviation for the state, and use the five-digit +4 for the ZIP if you have it.

**Some Thoughts on Titles**
- If you know that the person prefers to be addressed as "Dr." or "Ms.," you should do so. Always use a title of respect.
- You will want to add any titles such as "Dr." or "Ms." if sending to an elderly person or someone in a position of authority to show respect.
- If you know the person is married, use "Mrs." The same goes for "Dr." instead of "Ms." Or "The Honorable" for U.S. officials both present and past.

Here are some guidelines for titles (which can get tricky) right out of Emily Post.
**Addressing a Woman**
- Maiden name
Ms. Jane Johnson
Miss Jane Johnson*
*usually "Miss" is for girls under 18

- Married, keeping maiden name

Ms. Jane Johnson

- Married, uses husband's name socially

Mrs. John Kelly
Mrs. Jane Kelly*
*Nowadays this is acceptable
Ms. Jane Kelly

- Separated, not divorced

Mrs. John Kelly
Mrs. Jane Kelly
Ms. Jane Kelly

- Divorced

Mrs. Jane Kelly
Ms. Jane Kelly
Ms. Jane Johnson (maiden name)

- Widowed

Mrs. John Kelly*
*If you don't know the widow's preference, this is the traditional and preferred form
Mrs. Jane Kelly
Ms. Jane Kelly

Note: Traditionally, a woman's name preceded a man's on an envelope address, and his first and surname were not separated (Jane and John Kelly). Nowadays, the order of the names — whether his name or hers comes first — does not matter and either way is acceptable. The exception is when one member of the couple "outranks" the other — the one with the higher rank is always listed first.

- Married, she prefers Ms.

Mr. John Kelly and Ms. Jane Kelly

Ms. Jane Kelly and Mr. John Kelly

*Do not link Ms. to the husband's name:

Mr. and Ms. John Kelly is incorrect

- Married, she uses her husband's name socially

Jane and John Kelly

John and Jane Kelly

Mr. and Mrs. John Kelly

Or Dr. and Mrs. John Kelly

- Married, she uses maiden name

Mr. John Kelly and Ms. Jane Johnson

Ms. Jane Johnson and Mr. John Kelly

- If you can't fit the names on one line:

Mr. John Kelly

   and Ms. Jane Johnson (note the indent)

- Unmarried, living together

Mr. John Kelly & Ms. Jane Johnson

Note: Use one line

- A woman who outranks her husband:
  elected office, military rank

The Honorable Jane Kelly and Mr. John Kelly

If you can't fit both names on one line (note indent):

The Honorable Jane Kelly

   and Mr. John Kelly

- A woman who outranks her husband:
  professional or educational degree

Dr. Jane Kelly and Mr. John Kelly

- Both are doctors (medical or Ph.D.) and use the
  same last name

The Doctors Kelly (omit first names)

Drs. Jane and John Kelly / Drs. John and Jane Kelly

Dr. John Kelly and Dr. Jane Kelly / Dr. Jane Kelly and Dr. John Kelly

- Both are doctors (medical or Ph.D.), she uses her maiden name

Dr. Jane Johnson and Dr. John Kelly
Dr. John Kelly and Dr. Jane Johnson

**Business**
- Woman

Ms. is the default form of address, unless you know positively that a woman wishes to be addressed as Mrs.

- Professional designations — use only for business

Jane Kelly, CPA
Note: Do not use Ms. or Mr. if using a professional designation.
Socially, drop the professional designation and use Mr., Ms., or Mrs.: Ms. Jane Kelly

- Esquire:

Attorneys and some court officials
Jane Kelly, Esquire
Note: If using Esquire, do not use Ms. or Mr.
In conversation or socially, "Esquire" is not used; use Mr. or Ms.: Ms. Jane Kelly

Attorney at Law
Ms. Jane Kelly
Attorney at Law
This is an alternative to "Esquire" for attorneys. Use Mr. or Ms. and use two lines with no indent

## Same Sex

Write the names of both members of a same-sex couple on one line (for example, "Mr. Robert Pierce and Mr. Sean Harrison").

Another thoughtful consideration is when a woman lives alone and prefers not to have her full first name on the outside of an envelope. In that case, use an initial, such as "M. Jones." This makes the gender less specific and gives the person a more secure feeling of anonymity.

If the recipient is living in someone else's home or you have concerns that the U.S. Postal Service may not deliver mail to an unfamiliar name, add a note beneath the recipient's name such as "C/O James Gordon" on the line beneath "Maddie Thomas."

## Postage

Postage goes in the upper right-hand corner of the envelope across from the return address. Why do I add this detail? You won't believe how some of the stamps are affixed on envelopes addressed to me!

## Business Letter Rules

For business correspondence, use the same guidelines as above but add a couple other pieces of information. After the recipient's name, add his or her position, such as "Director of Sales." Try to do this on the same line as the name, but if there isn't enough room, you may move the title down to the next line. Beneath that, add the name of the company, followed by the address as directed in the guidelines above. If you're unsure of the recipient's name, you may write "Attn: Director of Sales."

## Mail to Overseas Military Installations

When sending a letter to a person in the military stationed overseas, use the same guidelines with a few additions. You'll want to add the recipient's rank and full name. The unit or squadron number should go on the second line. The next line should include APO or FPO, according to where the person is stationed, followed by the abbreviation of the region. The last line should include the name or abbreviation of the country in caps. Always add the full postal code to make sure it reaches the intended destination.

## Address Rules for Mailing to Other Countries

The general rules for addressing an envelope for a European destination are similar. Start with the recipient's name and title on the first line, followed by the street address on the second, the city, province or state with the postal code on the next line. The last line should have the name of the country in all caps. Beneath your return address, you should include "U.S.A."

## 70
## Won't You Share with Me Your Own Seeds of Awareness?

I was privileged to have coffee recently with a friend who had just returned from a trip to Maui.

She's a writer, and she shared with me a chance meeting she had with another writer — a poet and photographer/artist — while on vacation. This other writer was part of the crew on a boat that takes people snorkeling in the islands. Like so many writers, he has to supplement his income, because his books don't always support him as he requires.

In a conversation with this crew member, my friend discovered he was also a published author. At the end of the boat trip, he asked her to wait while he jumped ashore and ran to his locker. He returned with a beautiful book, *Seeds of Awareness – A Journey Towards Self Realization*, and gave it to her as a gift.

She was astounded at being given this beautiful book from its author.

In it, the author, Bob Pedersen, wrote:

Absolute knowledge
Existing
In the Mind of any One Person

243

will Find
Its Sheltered Existence
To be

—

Absolute

—

In that Place
And
That Place Alone

Had my friend not been open to sharing her own experiences, she would have never discovered Bob's book, his poetry or his art.

This sparked a conversation within me about why it is so important for us to share our knowledge with each other.

I write about topics that I feel are important to share. Things that I think will give other people an advantage. Things that I have learned through experience. Some of it is common sense. Some of it is from my own mistakes.

Most frequently, it is useful information that others have shared with me.

Which leads me to my point. Won't your share your knowledge with me? I think it important that I hear back from you, and that you share your stories, your truths. What have you learned through experience that might help others? What might prevent another from making the same mistakes or shield someone else from hurt?

So share with me, through email (johnkeyclass@gmail.com) or on The Key Class Web site (thekeyclass.com). With your permission, it would be great to print some of your stories, either crediting you or leaving them anonymous, whichever you prefer. You will just need to let me know your preferences.

I look forward to our future conversations so that what you have learned won't remain in "its sheltered existence to be absolute in that place and that place alone."

## 71
## When Are White Lies Acceptable?

Earlier in this book, I wrote an article about lying. In it, I touched upon "white lies." Here's what I wrote:

> We've all told white lies because brutal honesty might inflict pain or distress on another. For instance, Mary told Tim she couldn't go out with him on Saturday night because she and her family were going out of town. You are Mary's best friend and know it is because she doesn't find Tim attractive and doesn't want to date him.

> When Tim asks you if the reason is genuine, what do you say? Do you want to be brutally honest and tell Tim the truth or tell him you don't know if it is genuine or not to spare Tim's feelings? Perhaps in this instance it is better to be economical with the truth and just say you think Mary has other plans. This isn't the complete truth, but you are sparing Tim's feelings on something that won't have a real impact on his future.

> However, this is one of those instances where you need to clearly think it through. Some would advise you to very gently let Tim know that Mary isn't

really interested in him rather than saying something that will make matters worse. While you never want to hurt someone, there may be a diplomatic solution in which you tell Tim the truth and let Mary know about the conversation. She will probably be grateful that you ended her white lie, and both parties can move on with their lives.

.

What I wrote may be well and good, but it's been nagging at me. It's not a complete answer. I may not have the answer here, but let's look at some real-life situations where telling white lies may be the kind thing to do.

- A relative bakes her chocolate chip cookies and brings them to every family special occasion. The cookies are *terrible*. But, the relative is so proud of her cookies that no one has the heart or the guts to tell her the truth. In this case, sparing the relative's feelings is more important than telling the truth.

- A friend gets a terrible haircut. When you are asked what you think, rather than making your friend feel embarrassed or horrible about himself, you can say, "It's a change! What do you think?" Or, you can simply say "I like really short hair." Brutal honesty can be toxic. Never feel obligated to tell the *whole truth* when you know it will make someone ashamed of the way he or she looks.

- If you have done a huge favor for a friend or family member, and they thank you, rather than go into detail about the difficulties you had implementing the favor, simple say, "Oh, it was no trouble at all." Telling the person how much they put you out will only worry and upset them. Why do that? It's over and done with.

- When a child excitedly talks about Santa Claus or the Easter Bunny, feel free to protect the child's innocence and creative imagination by not fessing up that they don't exist!

- It's also okay to over-exaggerate when complimenting someone. For instance, I always told my mother that her macaroni and cheese was the best in the world!" It was exceptional, but best in the world might have been only in my eyes. This is a mild false truth that makes it easier for people to get along and is basically harmless in most cases.

The major difference between a white lie and a hard lie is that a hard lie is said to protect oneself, whereas a little white lie is said to protect someone else. Relationships can be complex and tricky at times. Sometimes a harmless, thoughtful pleasantry is just what the doctor ordered, especially when it saves others from minor hurt, shame or embarrassment.

Oftentimes, some of us tell a white lie to protect ourselves or others from punishment or disapproval for a minor failing or blunder which hurts nobody. This is borderline but okay as long as it doesn't hurt anyone.

**When Are White Lies Unacceptable**

White lies cross over into the dark side when we tell them to make us appear better than we really are or to protect some gain acquired previously for which we really aren't entitled. This happens at work often and falls under the category of taking credit for someone else's hard work, getting a promotion because of it, and then making sure the originator of the work is either suppressed or eventually fired to cover up the lie. This is no longer a white lie but rather a big, black one.

Lies that hurt someone else so that you can gain or that make others do something that would benefit you while harming themselves or causing themselves a loss never fall under the "white lie" scenario. Here we are into deceit, willful malice and sociopathic behavior!

It is not my purpose to give anyone a green light for telling lies. However, always weigh the harm being brutally honest with someone will do to others. And avoid anything that can seriously damage another.

# 72
## The Office Romance Mindfield

*Note: Jeanne Nelson, friend and colleague of PROWESS Workshops, wrote a fine piece on office romance. With her permission, I'm sharing it with you.*

**Birds do it**
**Bees do it**
**With each other employees do it**
**They do it, they fall in love.**

The Obamas did it. The Gateses did it. Even Michael Kors and Lance LaPere did. They fell in love while working together. And, everything seems to have worked out well for these former workplace lovebirds.

At the other end of the spectrum lives and careers have been left in ruins. Remember NASA astronauts Lisa Nowak and William Oefelein? Or the sensational criminal case involving former Detroit Mayor Kwame Kilpatrick and his former top aide Christine Beatty, who were involved in an extramarital workplace affair? And the equally sensational end to former New Jersey Governor Jim McGreevy's administration due to an extramarital affair with a subordinate?

249

On the lighter side, there are the workplace romances of our favorite TV characters over the years, some more successful than others. A few that come to mind are those of Jim Halpert-Pam Beesley, Diane Chambers and Sam Malone, and Maddie Hayes and David Addison.

**Are Office Romances On The Rise?**

The number of office romances appears to be on the rise. A survey by Vault.com found that more than half of its respondents engaged in an office romance. With young single Millennials entering the workplace and longer workdays becoming the norm, romance is bound to bloom. At least it will appear that way, as Millennials are far less concerned than Gen Xers and Boomers about keeping their office romances secret from coworkers and managers. But the Vault.com survey also revealed that the prevalence of office romances could relate to your profession or the industry in which you work.

However, while the Vault survey claims that "People in retail are the most likely to hook up at work, with 62% saying they had had office romances," an article in *BloombergBusiness* presents "a case for the decline in office romances due to 'the rise of the retaliation lawsuit.'"

**Four Types of Office Romances**
- **Classic Romance** - Two single coworkers are attracted to each other. Whether that relationship ends up in marriage or in a breakup, the initial intent was innocent.
- **Extramarital Affair** - One or both coworkers are married and wind up cheating on their marriage partners.
- **Fling** - Two coworkers -- single or married -- are attracted to each other on a purely sexual basis and engage in a one-night-stand, often prompted by a business trip, industry event or

annual Christmas party. There is usually no intention of becoming serious, but a "coworkers with benefits" relationship might ensue that involves casual sex as opportunities arise.

- **Don Juan Syndrome** - Usually a male coworker whose aim is sexual conquests. He will flirt with female coworkers, often new or young unsuspecting victims, with the express intent to bed them and move on.

## Who Gets Hurt In An Office Romance?

According to a 2014 Harris Poll conducted for CareerBuilder, nearly a third of office romances ended in marriage. That leaves two-thirds of office romances vulnerable to professional and personal complications. And, who gets hurt?

Several decades ago, it was women who were hurt the most in office romances and affairs because they were (a) usually in subordinate positions (but not always) and considered to be less valuable employees, (b) not confident or supported enough by their companies or the law to stand up for themselves and (c) because filing charges often resulted in professional reputational loss and backlash. Even today women are usually viewed through a different and more critical eye than men. Companies often will make financial settlements with women out of court to keep the allegations confidential; but this still can hurt women professionally while failing to solve the problem of sexual harassment in their companies. And, shockingly, the lawyer a woman might turn to for help could be guilty of sexual harassment himself or herself, or his or her firm might discourage women from pursuing the same legal course as they encourage their clients to pursue!

Of course, men can get hurt as well, as we've seen from the examples previously provided. Men who hold senior

251

positions are especially vulnerable: CEOs, politicians, celebrities and the like. But among average employees, including middle managers, women continue to be judged more harshly than men when in an office romance, especially if she is involved with a man who is above her pay grade.

Companies themselves can also be hurt through reputational loss, sexual harassment claims, and lawsuits. With more awareness of the laws that protect all employees from sexual harassment -- often a byproduct of the office romance -- companies are finding themselves in defensive mode. As a result, more companies are making policies regarding employees dating each other and sometimes applying as well to married couples working together in the same area or even at the same company.

### How to Avoid / Manage an Office Romance

People will continue to be attracted to each other anywhere, anytime. It's not unusual for coworkers on average to spend more time with each other than they spend with their families and friends; thus, it's likely that they will fall in and out of love a lot. And the impact of those workplace romances is felt by other coworkers and can disrupt the office routine. So while employers and ethicists debate whether or not to ban romance from the office, the following are some steps to avoid or manage your office romance:

- *Check your company's policy regarding dating coworkers* and married couples working together. Think about what you would do if you were attracted to a coworker and how you would manage a romantic relationship at your place of work. This should include your exit strategies.
- *Exit Strategy No. 1*: Plan how you would end the romance, and handle any unpleasant aftermath such as an unprofessional attitude or even harassment from your ex-lover.

252

- ***Exit Strategy No. 2:*** Plan how you will find a new job within the company, away from your ex-romantic partner, or at another company, state, country, planet, etc., if -- and more likely when -- your romance ends. Working together while being involved is hard; working together after the breakup is harder.
- ***Avoid like the plague an affair with a married coworker.*** If *you're* the married coworker, think twice about stepping over that line. It could be fatal to your job, career and marriage. Adultery is illegal in 23 U.S. states, so keep that in mind as well.
- ***Discourage a coworker politely, or not so politely***, when you are not interested. Leading someone on because you can't say "no" clearly can create a sticky situation, and you won't even have the benefit of being in love for your trouble.
- ***Avoid becoming involved with someone who is not your peer***; that means nix to your boss or other organizational superiors, or with someone who is below your pay grade or subordinate to you. The odds are against a good outcome and could set up a sexual harassment situation.
- ***Avoid, if possible, dating a coworker in your immediate department.*** Dating a coworker from another department with whom you have some work distance can reduce the strain.
- ***If you are attracted to a single coworker and Cupid strikes***, take it slow so you can keep professional control over the situation while you determine the potential for it turning serious or permanent.

- *Consider notifying your boss, or respective bosses, and HR* if it appears that your romance is the real thing and could become permanent. But, one or both of you should be prepared to transfer to other areas, either to comply with corporate policy or to accommodate your current department. Being on the up and up is likely to garner respect from HR, your manager(s) and your team. And, taking the initiative shows that you both are trustworthy and responsible, and allows the two of you to maintain some control over your jobs and relationship. But, these steps require your judgment call.
- *Refrain from hanging around your coworker* boyfriend or girlfriend excessively at work, especially at the expense of getting your work done. You will look foolish on several counts.
- *Don't show favoritism to your office lover.* Such actions could not only ruin your reputation and stunt your advancement, but depending on the situation, serious complaints or even legal action could be lodged against you. Conversely, discourage your romantic partner from doing the same with you.
- *Go public as soon as possible.* Don't kid yourselves that others are in the dark about your relationship. They aren't. Nobody is.
- *Handle the breakup with dignity, grace and maturity.* Follow the plan you laid out in the beginning; if necessary, transfer to another department or find a job with another company. Whatever you do, don't spread your heartbreak and baggage around your office. You can survive, and thrive.

254

*See Jeanne Nelson's original article via http://www.prowessworkshops.com/blog/the-office-romance-minefield.html for all resources used in this article.*

# 73
# What Makes a Great Team?

A team can't flourish and thrive without a great team leader, a leader that is a role model who simultaneously gives its team members room to breathe. Room to grow. Room to relate.

## Where to Start?
- Start by introducing yourself. Share your history. Explain:
- How and where you learned from your success.
- How and where you learned from your failures.
- Be open to sharing.
- Explain your management style.
- Then, explain your style of being a team player.

## What Characteristics Should You Possess?
- Never give orders in a "talk-down-to" attitude.
- Always offer suggestions for doing something a better way rather than saying "you are wrong; do it this way."
- Understand that the best way to get positive results is to say, "Would you be willing to…?" This will yield positive results.
- NEVER call someone down in front of others.

- ALWAYS praise in front of others.
- ALWAYS have a positive attitude.
- Never underestimate what your actions will do to affect team members and the ultimate client.
- Treat everyone with empathy.
- Encourage your team to treat others with empathy.
- Understand that each person's reality is his or her own. People see and feel each situation differently. You cannot change how they feel.

## How Do I Encourage Positive Results?

- Encourage an open door policy with your team.
- Schedule a 15-minute meeting at the end of each week to discuss the good and the bad of the week.   Discuss alternative actions to general or specific procedures.
- Don't assign blame to people but rather look at why certain methodology or behavior didn't succeed.
- To get people to dress and act and speak kindly with others, be a role model for them, not a dictator. Dress, act and speak as you want them to do, and they will model their behavior after yours.
- Leave your ego behind. There is no ego in a successful team.
- Respect everyone. Treat no one differently.
- Prevent disrespect in the workplace. Make sure that team members are "Upstanders" not "Bystanders. A bystander doesn't show empathy or stand up for others. If they see bullying in the workplace, they don't report it. Their actions affect others. But, Upstanders stand up for others; report any suspicious incidents of abuse or bullying and make friends

257

with the underdog. Their actions can change the lives of others.

## "You will never treat anyone here differently because of who they love, how they dress, or what their body looks like." –Sean Kosofsky

Follow the link to Sean Kosofsky's video, "The Most Beautiful Way to Stop a Bully I've ever Seen"[28] in the Video Resources Section.

### Why Does This Work?

This works because behavior trickles down. If you are polite and respectful at all costs, your team will be too. Demonstrate and encourage respect for all, no matter what you do or where you are.

# 74
# How to Be at the Top of Your Game ... and Know when You Are Not

Not long ago I signed with a service provider to work with me on The Key Class. By "service provider," I don't mean an Internet service, but someone to help me accomplish my goals with my company.

After the first initial meetings, I was so excited and ready to go. I was given lots of ideas on what I needed to be doing ... but after about a month or so ... I realized that nothing that had been promised on the other end of the relationship was being delivered.

I had that sinking feeling in the pit of my stomach that I'd made a mistake. Another few months later and that feeling became a reality. So rather than let it go on, I decided to own my mistake and correct it. That led to a meeting where I determined with the provider that we both had a lack of understanding of each other's needs. As a result, we terminated our agreement.

So onward and upward. About a month ago, I found someone else to fulfill the services that I so desperately needed. I signed the dotted line and held my breath. Within two days, my inbox was inundated with positive accomplished tasks! By the end of the first two weeks, this person had accomplished more than her predecessor had in three months! I was in heaven, and still am.

But, what makes the difference between someone who talks a good game compared to someone who is at the top of her game?

- Excellent time management
- Fine-tuned organizational skills
- Attention to detail
- Delivering more than is promised
- Great and continuous communication
- Providing quality work in a time-efficient manner
- Keeping a positive, upbeat attitude
- Dealing with others with respect
- Always maintaining a courteous, friendly manner in person, on the phone and via email
- Handling all issues in a highly-ethical manner
- Taking responsibility for your actions
- Being a team player – there is no "i" in team.

I could go on, but I think you get the picture. It's one thing to be personable enough to win a contract with a client. It's another thing to uphold your end of the bargain. Whether you make that bargain with an employer or as an independent contractor, if you want to build a great reputation and assure yourself of long-term or repeat business, these are the skills to keep in mind. Talent and skill are merely the basic price of entry. How you deliver them involves soft skills that will be the critical difference between your success and failure in the eyes of others.

# CONCLUSION

I have learned the true meaning of the phrase, "You have to live it to understand it."

In the pages of this collection of articles, you have seen a true demonstration of that phrase. I have had both the pleasure and misfortune of living through just about every situation about which I've written. I hope that this collection will support all of you, young or old, to live a happier and more successful life. Success, to me, does not equal dollar signs necessarily. It is a matter of waking up in the morning and looking at yourself in the mirror and knowing the person looking back at you is a good person that feels fulfilled with his or her life.

As you have seen in my writing and if you have ever heard me speak, you know that I believe if you find something that you love to do, you will never go to work a day in your life. I spent 44 years in the event industry and can say that I feel I went to work for a total of 1 ½ years. Those 1 ½ years were spent on employee issues and dealing with the government in one manner or another. The remaining 42 ½ years were pure love. I could not wait to wake up in the morning and go to the next project. Imagine the thrill for a high school graduate to travel the world and fulfill all of his wildest fantasies for events on someone else's dollar, and get paid for it!

Now that I have retired from that world, I have found another wonderful career that I cannot wait to wake up for each morning. Teaching the skills of a better life to young and old is one of the most rewarding things I have ever done. To see the light come on in someone's eyes tells me that person "got" my message, and trust me, it's a privileged experience that everyone should have.

If there is one story or point that has hit you as an "a-ha moment," then I have succeeded with this book. I hope you have enjoyed learning from my experiences. Now, please pay it forward. The world will be a better place for it; I promise.

**THE END**

## ABOUT THE AUTHOR

The Key Class founder, John J. Daly, Jr., was a highly-successful international event producer who advised his Fortune 100 corporate clients on proper protocol both in the U.S. and around the globe for 44 years.

In 2010, based on his 20-year experience of mentoring youth who demonstrated extremely poor social and dining skills, John founded and created The Key Class for high school and college students. He began by teaching The Key Class through the Santa Barbara Teen Court, which he has continued for the past five years. Since 2013, Daly has provided the program to multiple high schools in Santa Barbara and currently has expanded it to all high schools in the Santa Barbara Unified School District. In addition, he teaches The Key Class through the Workforce Investment Board, United Way and a number of other organizations.

In 2013-14, John Daly won the "Outstanding Fun In the Stun Individual Partner of the Year" Award from United Way. The same year, Daly won "mentor of the year" from Santa Barbara High School's Dons Net Café and the 2014 Penny Jenkins Mentor Champion Award from the Fighting

Back Mentor Program. John is the 2015-2016 President of Partners in Education.

This book is a sequel to *The Key Class – The Keys to Job Search Success*, which remains popular through Amazon.com, BarnesandNoble.com, Kobo and SmashWords.

# REFERENCES

## In order of Reference

10, 11, 12 129
Andrea Michaels:
http://www.extraordinaryevents.net/pages-about/bio-andrea.html
http://www.extraordinaryevents.net/

17, 18
Stageoflife.com:
http://www.stageoflife.com/

17
PRWeb:
http://www.prweb.com/releases/etiquette/statistics/prweb11542968.htm

17
Statistics About Teens:
http://www.stageoflife.com/StageHighSchool/OtherResources/Statistics_on_High_School_Students_and_Teenagers.aspx

18
Stageoflife.com Winning Essay:
http://www.stageoflife.com/Default.aspx?tabid=72&g=posts&t=11808

24
Survey on Bad Manners:
http://www.schools.com/visuals/bad-manners.html

39, 187
Carol McKibben:
http://www.carolmckibben.com
http://www.carolmckibben.com/blog

40
Napoleon Hill:
http://www.amazon.com/Think-Grow-Rich-
Napoleon-Hill/dp/1453670114

42
NBA.com:
http://www.nba.com

42
*Sports Illustrated:*
http://www.si.com/

42
*New York Times:*
http://www.nytimes.com/

42
Joseph Walker:
http://topics.wsj.com/person/W/joseph-walker/7751

42
*The Wall Street Journal*:
http://www.wsj.com/
http://www.wsj.com/articles/SB10001424052748704
182004575055191587179832

43
Mark Cuban's Blog:
http://markcubanblog.com/

43
*Fortune*:
http://fortune.com/

43
Gawker:
http://gawker.com/

47
SuccessConsciousness.com:
http://www.successconsciousness.com/

48
The Simple Dollar:
http://www.thesimpledollar.com/

56
Dale Partridge:
http://dalepartridge.com/my-story/
http://dalepartridge.com/

58
Roz Usheroff:
https://remarkableleader.wordpress.com/meet-roz-usheroff/
https://www.linkedin.com/pulse/four-steps-overcoming-disappointment-roz-usheroff
https://remarkableleader.wordpress.com/2015/01/29/how-to-make-2015-your-breakout-year/

63
The Women's Conference:
http://www.womensconference.org/home.html

66
How to Be a Friend to a Friend Who's Sick:
http://www.amazon.com/How-Be-Friend-Whos-Sick/dp/1610392833/ref=sr_1_1?ie=UTF8&qid=1389116496&sr=8-1&keywords=How+to+be+a+friend+to+a+friend+who%2527s+sick

69
Leah Polakoff at Pennilive:
http://www.pennlive.com/

75
Julie Blais Comeau's article: "Sticky Situations: Saying No to Charity":
http://www.huffingtonpost.ca/julie-blais-comeau/charity-etiquette-_b_1229808.html

80
Abuse Information and Help:
How to Help Someone Who Is Being Abused
http://www.emergecenter.org/get-help/how-to-help-someone-who-is-being-abused/
How to Help a Friend Who Is Being Abused
https://www.womenshealth.gov/violence-against-women/get-help-for-violence/how-to-help-a-friend-who-is-being-abused.html
Help a Loved One or Friend
http://abuseintervention.org/help/friend-family/
Recognizing, Preventing and Reporting Child Abuse
http://www.helpguide.org/articles/abuse/child-abuse-and-neglect.htm

89
Dr. Randall S. Hansen:
http://www.quintcareers.com/web_master.html
http://www.quintcareers.com/job_skills_values.html

87
Dr. Katharine Hansen:
http://www.quintcareers.com/creative_director.html
http://www.quintcareers.com/job_skills_values.html

89
Employability Skills Assessment:
http://www.quintcareers.com/employability_skills_as
sessment.html

97
Susan M. Heathfield:
http://humanresources.about.com/bio/Susan-M-
Heathfield-6016.htm

101
Amy Rees Anderson:
http://www.amyreesanderson.com/about.html

105
*60 Minutes:*
*http://www.cbsnews.com/60-minutes/*

105
Bonnie Siegel:
http://eventplanningexperts.com/who-we-are/meet-
the-team/

105
ASE Group:
http://www.ase-group.com/

106
Bill Taylor:
http://williamctaylor.com/about-bill/

106
Fast Company:
http://www.fastcompany.com/

106
Harvard Business Review:
https://hbr.org/

106
Arkadi Kuhlmann:
http://en.wikipedia.org/wiki/Arkadi_Kuhlmann

106
ING Direct USA:
http://www.ing.com/en.htm

106
Raj Sheth, Recruiterbox:
http://recruiterbox.com/

106
ere.net:
http://www.ere.net/

107
Career Advisory Board:
http://careeradvisoryboard.org/

107
LeadershipIQ:
http://www.leadershipiq.com/

107
John Myrna:
http://myrna.com/About

114
Beth Braccio Hering
CareerBuilder.com:
CareerBuilder.com

114
Lisa Quast:
Career Woman Inc. –
http://www.careerwomaninc.com

115
Roy Cohen:
*The Wall Street Professional's Survival Guide*
http://www.amazon.com/Wall-Street-
Professional%C2%BFs-Survival-
Guide/dp/0137052642

115
Brad Karsh:
http://jbtrainingsolutions.com

121
Barbara Pachter:
https://www.americanexpress.com/us/small-
business/openforum/articles/can-polite-people-be-
successful-leaders/

121
The Essentials of Business Etiquette:
http://www.pachter.com

121
Vivian Giang:
http://www.viviangiang.com/

127
"When Is a Contract Not a Contract?"
http://worldofextraordinaryevents.blogspot.com/

129
"Demystifying the Proposal Process and Winning Business without Losing Money"
http://worldofextraordinaryevents.blogspot.com/2015/01/rfps-demystifying-process-and-win-business.html

*138*
*Business News Daily:*
http://www.businessnewdaily.com

142
Jack Canfield:
*Key to Living the Law of Attraction: A simple guide in Creating the Life of Your Dreams*
http://www.amazon.com/Jack-Canfields-Key-Living-Attraction/dp/0757306586

144
Greg Baker of Advance Consulting:
http://www.advanceconsulting.com/blog/conflict-management-how-to-avoid-being-thrown-under-the-bus-2/

165
Bruce Kasanoff:
http://kasanoff.com/about/

177
*New York Daily News:*
http://www.nydailynews.com/

177
Ohio State University:
https://www.osu.edu/

177
The Daily Mail:
http://www.dailymail.co.uk/ushome/index.html

101, 178
*Forbes*:
http://www.forbes.com/
http://www.forbes.com/fdc/welcome_mjx.shtml

http://www.forbes.com/2010/06/16/office-romance-relationship-breakup-forbes-woman-leadership-workplace.html

180
Pepperdine University:
http://www.pepperdine.edu/

181
Graziadio School of Business and Management:
http://bschool.pepperdine.edu/

182
Space Shuttle *Columbia:*
http://www.nasa.gov/centers/kennedy/shuttleoperatio
ns/orbiters/orbiterscol.html

197
Mindtools:
http://www.mindtools.com/page8.html?

198
Kenneth W. Thomas:
http://faculty.nps.edu/vitae/cgi-
bin/vita.cgi?p=display_vita&id=1023567855

198
Ralph Kilmann:
http://www.kilmanndiagnostics.com/ralph-h-kilmann

198
The Thomas-Kilmann Conflict Mode Instrument:
http://www.kilmanndiagnostics.com/catalog/thomas-
kilmann-conflict-mode-instrument

202
Active Listening Skills/MindTools:
http://www.mindtools.com/CommSkll/ActiveListenin
g.htm

203
Assertive Approach:
http://www.mindtools.com/pages/article/Assertivenes
s.htm

204
Win-Win Negotiation:
http://www.mindtools.com/CommSkll/NegotiationSki
lls.htm

206, 249
Jeanne Nelson:
http://www.prowessworkshops.com/the-instructor/
http://www.prowessworkshops.com/

214
Dr. Barton Goldsmith:
http://www.drbartongoldsmith.com/

219
Beth Cooper-Zobott:
http://www.equityapartments.com/

220
Brian Monahan:
Prestige AV & Creative Services
http://www.prestigeav.com/

223
National Do Not Call Registry:
https://www.donotcall.gov/

231
Marion Grobb Finkelstein:
http://www.marionspeaks.com/

237
Emily Post:
http://www.emilypost.com/

243
Bob Pedersen
*Seeds of Awareness – A Journey Towards Self
Realization*
http://www.amazon.com/Seeds-Awareness-Bob-
Pedersen/dp/0974416304/ref=sr_1_1?ie=UTF8&qid=
1434993488&sr=8-
1&keywords=Seeds+of+Awareness+by+Bob+Peders
en&pebp=1434993491782&perid=0AXT2PGZH210
GCYX3C8M

250
Vault Survey:
http://www.vault.com/blog/workplace-issues/2015-
office-romance-survey-results/

249-255
Workplace Ethics Advice:
http://www.workplaceethicsadvice.com/2014/02/the-
dangers-of-workplace-dating.html

249-255
References for The Office Romance Mindfield
http://www.prowessworkshops.com/blog/the-office-
romance-minefield.html

# VIDEO RESOURCES

1. Disarming Techinques:
   https://www.youtube.com/watch?v=C43FhOz pmHI

2. Rudeness in America:
   https://www.youtube.com/watch?v=jooJnhgS gIA

3. Respect:

   https://www.youtube.com/watch?v=DOvZLOL9zd0

4. How to handle chronically late employees:
   http://www.noozhawk.com/article/john_daly_t he_consequences_of_being_late_20140722

5. How to make others feel important:
   https://www.youtube.com/watch?t=13&v=- PURfoGn4yw

6. The Women's Conference:
   https://www.youtube.com/watch?v=qZEuzXX YQzc

7. Sidewalk Etiquette, on Video:
   https://www.youtube.com/watch?v=_fUqvyrL A_M

8. The Art of Saying "No":
   https://www.youtube.com/watch?v=AqN9jcL A61s

9. How Can You Match Your Personal Qualities to the Job?

https://www.youtube.com/watch?v=cmIH5Co aaGs

10. How to Practice Proper Business Meeting Etiquette: https://www.youtube.com/watch?v=15Av0DL UQNk

11. Unethical Behavior: https://www.youtube.com/watch?v=2z_XeVC nQy8

12. What Makes Unethical Behavior Contagious: http://www.amyreesanderson.com/about.html

13. Do Managers Hire for Attitude or Aptitude? https://www.youtube.com/watch?v=Y6Wg6K 3qXbI

14. Gossip in the Workplace: https://www.youtube.com/watch?v=HoYExK hIwU4

15. How to Practice Good Etiquette in Your Cubicle: https://www.youtube.com/watch?v=E9Io2RE DPVQ

16. 6 Ways to Get an Angry Customer to Back Down: https://www.youtube.com/watch?v=ACKbkm O9rLg

17. How to Quit Your Job: Resigning with Class: https://www.youtube.com/watch?v=pv0sRyLt q2s

18. Amy Cuddy: Your Body Language Shapes Who You Are:

https://www.youtube.com/watch?v=Ks-_Mh1QhMc

19. How to Shake Hands and Introduce Yourself:
https://www.youtube.com/watch?v=41BdlgNyKFI

20. How to Create a Hot Personal Brand:
https://www.youtube.com/watch?v=z_fIsyOFrKQ

21. Phone Etiquette Training:
https://www.youtube.com/watch?v=54xYxV1SoaU

22. Office Email Etiquette:
https://www.youtube.com/watch?v=MVHQs8Gi9KM

23. Texting While Walking:
https://www.youtube.com/watch?v=wl0JojWH1rQ
https://www.youtube.com/watch?v=pLA1UelcDrE

24. Elevator Speech Examples:
http://speakingppt.com/2012/07/26/3-best-elevator-pitches/
http://elevatorspeechexamples.com/
https://www.youtube.com/watch?v=y1Y02_oZP8U

25. Conversation Etiquette:
https://www.youtube.com/watch?v=JwcOX43gLyc

26. How to Keep Your Audience's Attention:
    https://www.youtube.com/watch?v=SbSDUO
AuQO8

27. How to Write a Proper Email:
    https://www.youtube.com/watch?v=9TF7znkF
vd8

28. The Most Beautiful Way to Stop a Bully I've Ever Seen:
    https://drive.google.com/file/d/0B2sC2x41liY

    _QUNyV1JKSGc2V0E/view

    https://drive.google.com/file/d/0B2sC2x41liY

    _SDZ4T2hta3dQNU0/view?usp=sharing

www.ingramcontent.com/pod-product-compliance
Lightning Source LLC
La Vergne TN
LVHW051039080426
835508LV00019B/1610